BILINGUALISM
AND
LEARNING
DISABILITIES

BILINGUALISM AND LEARNING DISABILITIES

Policy and Practice for Teachers and Administrators

Edited by

Ann C. Willig, Ph.D.

Handicapped Minority Research Institute
University of Texas, Austin

and

Hinda F. Greenberg, M.L.S.

Manager, Information Center
The Carnegie Foundation for the Advancement of Teaching
Princeton, New Jersey

American Library
Publishing Co. Inc.

Copyright 1986 by American Library Publishing Co., Inc.

Published and distributed by
AMERICAN LIBRARY PUBLISHING CO., INC.
275 Central Park West
New York, N.Y. 10024

Printed and bound in U.S.A.

Cover Photo: Ms. Isabel Velazquez, Teacher, P.S. 145, Community School
District 3, Borough of Manhattan, New York City (Courtesy of Carmen Gloria
Burgos, Librarian, Office of Bilingual Education, New York City.)

Library of Congress Cataloging-in-Publication Data

Main entry under title:
Bilingualism and learning disabilities: Policy and practice for teachers and
administrators

Includes index.

1. Children of minorities — Education — United States — Addresses,
essays, lectures. 2. Learning disabilities — United States —
Addresses, essays, lectures. I. Willig, Ann C. (Cecelia).
II. Greenberg, Hinda Feige.

LC3731.B558   1986   371.97   85-28677
ISBN 0-934598-92-4 *(pbk.)*
ISBN 0-934598-95-9

CONTENTS

LIST OF CONTRIBUTORS

Alba N. Ambert participated in a study of language disorders and development in Spanish-speaking children as a visiting scientist in the Department of Linguistics at the Massachusetts Institute of Technology in 1985. Earlier, as a National Research Council Fellow, she served as Assistant Professor and Director of the Bilingual Special Education Teacher Training Program at the University of Hartford in Connecticut. *Bilingual Education: A Sourcebook,* which Dr. Ambert co-authored with S. E. Melendez, was published in 1985.

Angela Carrasquillo, a frequent speaker at professional conferences, is Associate Professor in the Division of Curriculum and Teaching at Fordham University in New York City. She is also Coordinator of the TESOL Program and Director of the Fordham University Puerto Rico Programs. Writing extensively in the areas of bilingual and language education and reading, Dr. Carrasquillo published her most recent book, *The Teaching of Reading in Spanish to the Bilingual Student,* in 1984.

Jim Cummins, Director of the National Heritage Language Resource Unit at the Ontario Institute for Studies in Education in Toronto, Canada, focuses his research on minority-group achievement, bilingualism, and reading disability. In 1979 Dr. Cummins and his co-author, J. P. Das, received the International Reading Association Albert J. Harris Award for their paper on the detection and remediation of reading disability. His book *Bilingualism and Special Education: Issues in Assessment and Pedagogy* was published in the United States in 1984.

Barbara M. Flores, Assistant Professor in the Department of Elementary Education at Arizona State University, has participated in action research for the past three years. Her major research areas include the development of language, literacy, and cognition.

Shernas Bathena Garcia is a Research Associate with the Undergraduate Bilingual Special Education Training Program at the University of Texas at Austin. Dr. Garcia has taught handicapped students and developed training materials for the education of the severely handicapped. She also has administered a federally funded office for research in Hispanic education and conducted research concerned with limited-English-proficient handicapped students in Texas.

Hinda Feige Greenberg, Co-Editor of this volume, former Associate Editor of the *Journal of Reading, Writing, and Learning Disabilities International* and Information Specialist at the Educational Testing Service, Princeton, New Jersey, is Manager, Information Center at The Carnegie Foundation for the Advancement of Teaching in Princeton, New Jersey.

Wayne H. Holtzman, Jr., is Coordinator of the Bilingual Special Education Master's Program at the University of Texas at Austin. He has taught courses concerned with assessment issues in bilingual special education at both the National University in Mexico City and UTA. As an associate of the Southwest Educational Development Laboratory, he has participated in NIE-sponsored bilingual in-service research projects.

Wesley A. Hoover's background is in psycholinguistics, research design, statistical analysis, and computer applications. Dr. Hoover is Senior Evaluator at the Southwest Educational Development Laboratory. Earlier, as Senior Research associate in the Division of Language and Literacy at the SEDL, he co-directed a longitudinal investigation on the relations between current schooling practices and the language and reading achievement of low-income Hispanic children. His publications include works on psycholinguistics, language proficiency evaluation, and bilingual education.

Betty J. Mace-Matluck, Senior Researcher for the School Improvement Services Group at the Southwest Educational Development Laboratory, has extensive experience in language and reading research and public school teaching, supervision, administration, and teacher training. She has directed several large field-based research projects on language proficiency testing, second-language acquisition, and the methods used to teach language-minority children. Her published works are in the fields of psycholinguistics, applied linguistics, and second-language education and assessment.

Elba Maldonado-Colon, Coordinator of the Bilingual Special Education Undergraduate Program at the University of Texas at Austin. Dr. Maldonado-Colon has spoken on communication-disordered Hispanic children, curriculum design and instructional intervention programs for exceptional bilingual students, first- and second-language acquisition, language assessment, and school-community involvement. She is also the author of several handbooks and training manuals for teachers of culturally and linguistically different students.

Alba A. Ortiz, Associate Professor in the Department of Special Education at the University of Texas at Austin, is the Director of both the Bilingual Special Education Department and the Handicapped Minority Research Institute of Language Proficiency at UTA. She was a member of the U.S. President's Committee on Mental Retardation and chairperson of the Minority Groups Committee of the Council for Exceptional Children. The author of many scholarly works, she will publish "Education of Culturally and Linguistically Different Children" in 1986.

Brenda Porter, a special education teacher in Tempe, Arizona, has participated in action research for the past two years. She is particularly interested in generating and refining research-based instructional practices that will enhance the development of language, literacy, and cognition in special education students.

Diana Rivera Viera, Associate Professor in the Special Education Program at the University of Puerto Rico, teaches doctoral courses in educational psychology at Temple University in Philadelphia in consortium with the Social Sciences Program of the University of Puerto Rico. President of the Puerto Rico chapter and a member of the Caribbean Committee of the International Reading Association, she has served as a consultant in bilingual education for both the Public School

System in Springfield, Massachusetts, and the Bilingual Education Council in Boston.

Robert Rueda, Associate Professor in the Department of Special Education at Arizona State University, is currently on leave at the Southwest Regional Laboratory in Los Alamitos, California. His primary research interests include social competence and social interaction and the interactional social aspects of learning and development in both bilingual and special education students.

Carmen Simich-Dudgeon is the ESL/special education resource teacher for the Fairfax County Public Schools in Virginia, Director of the Trinity-Arlington Parent-Teacher Training Demonstration Project, and a staff member of the Department of Education and Counseling, Trinity College, Washington, D.C. She specializes in program administration and evaluation, English proficiency assessment, and special and bilingual education.

Ann C. Willig, co-editor of this volume as well as a contributor to it, is Coordinator of longitudinal research at the Handicapped Minority Research Institute on Language Proficiency at the University of Texas at Austin. A graduate of the University of Puerto Rico, Dr. Willig has taught in both public and private Puerto Rican schools. Her M.S. degree in special education and Ph.D. in educational psychology, with a specialization in bilingual education, were received at the University of Illinois at Champaign-Urbana.

James R. Yates, Associate dean of the College of Education at the University of Texas at Austin, is also Professor in the departments of Special Education and Educational Administration. His areas of research include special education services to the handicapped, the use of technological forecasting methods in educational planning, and the financing of special education. His most recent publication, with co-author A. Ortiz, appears in *The Bilingual Special Education Interface* edited by L. M. Baca and H. T. Cervantes.

PREFACE

All but two of the twenty-five largest public school systems in this country presently have a majority of minority students enrolled. The largest ethnic groups are blacks, Mexican Americans, and Puerto Ricans. The latest census reveals Hispanics have shown the greatest population increase; not surprisingly, they have the lowest median age of the ethnic minority groups. This translates into the projection that there will be yet an increase in the Hispanic minority student enrollment in our public schools.

Bilingual minority students constitute an unusually high proportion of special educational classes. Why is this? Do these bilingual students truly have learning problems, or are they reflecting cultural and linguistic differences that are misunderstood? Who in the education community is fit to make such a decision? Who will train the decision-makers? What policy issues must be resolved before an accurate assessment, dominant-language based, and psychologically sound, can take place? What remediative measures can be implemented so that true language disorders can be corrected?

The contributors to this Supplement are eminently qualified to address these questions and propose solutions. It has been my pleasure to work with them; in so doing, I have been impressed with their personal commitment to the resolution of a dilemma that communities everywhere will soon face.

Hinda Feige Greenberg

INTRODUCTION

Among the millions of children in this country who were affected by the passage of PL 94-142, there are a substantial number whose language and culture differ from that of the dominant society. When Congress mandated the right to a free and appropriate public education for *all* handicapped children, with nondiscriminatory assessment, placement, and instructional procedures that would meet the unique educational needs of each exceptional child, the special needs of the culturally and linguistically different child became a focus of concern for many researchers and educators. Every facet and every level of educational planning and instruction for ethnic-minority children has been found to be fraught with complex issues and with challenges that must be faced by individual educators, administrators, and policy-makers. This and the next issue focus on the concerns of researchers and educators who are attempting to ensure that the unique educational needs of the culturally and linguistically different child in this country are met.

High on the list of priorities of those who are concerned about the quality of education offered to minority-group children in this country is the development of optimal instructional strategies, both for children who have demonstrated learning problems and for low-achieving children in the regular classroom. Programs developed for literacy acquisition in the bilingual child illustrate the implementation of an exciting new approach to reading instruction which utilizes the same natural developmental sequences that characterize language acquisition.

Hopefully, those who have not been introduced to the complexity of the issues that affect the education of culturally and linguistically different children will gain new insights and will be challenged to address those concerns presented here that are found within their own realm of endeavors.

Ann C. Willig

There are long-term positive effects among high school students who have participated in bilingual education programs. These students are achieving higher scores on tests of verbal and mathematical skills.

National Assessment of Educational Progress
National Center for Education Statistics—
High School and Beyond Studies
Survey of Income and Education

1

PSYCHOLOGICAL ASSESSMENT OF MINORITY STUDENTS:
Out of Context, Out of Focus, Out of Control?

Jim Cummins

For more than fifty years educators have pointed to the abuses of psychological tests when applied to students from cultural or linguistic minority groups (e.g., Mercer, 1973; Sanchez, 1934). These concerns finally found legal expression in 1975 with the passage of Public Law (PL) 94-142 which entailed what appeared to be strong provisions against discriminatory assessment.

Recent studies, however, suggest that even when PL 94-142 is implemented, discrimination still continues (Mehan, Hertweck and Meihls, in press; Ortiz and Yates, 1983). Ortiz and Yates, for example, reported that Hispanic students in Texas were over-represented by a factor of three hundred percent in the "learning disabilities" category. The ethnographic study conducted by Mehan, et al., found no empirical basis for teachers' referrals of students for psychological assessment. Yet, the referral exercised a major influence on the actual psychological assessment in that psychologists continued to test until they "found" the disability that could be invoked to "explain" the student's apparent academic difficulties.

A similar conclusion emerged from the analysis of more than four hundred psychological assessments of minority students conducted by Cummins (1984). Although no diagnostic conclusions were logically possible in the majority of assessments, psychologists were most reluctant to risk their professional credibility by admitting this fact to teachers and parents.

The argument in the present paper is that discriminatory assessment of minority students is virtually inevitable when the process focuses exclusively on the student and ignores the societal context within which minority students develop and schools attempt to educate. Legislation such as PL 94-142 is largely ineffective in altering discriminatory assessment procedures because it leaves essentially unchanged the *role relationships* between teachers, psychologists and students, on the one hand, and between schools and the minority communities they serve, on the other. Within this system of role relationships, the psychological assessment has operated to screen from critical scrutiny both the societal roots of minority students' academic difficulties and the educational treatment experienced by the child. This screening is achieved through the adoption of a medical model of assessment that necessitates that the "problem" be located within the child.

THE CONTEXT OF
MINORITY STUDENT ASSESSMENT

Typically, assessment procedures take little account of the context within which minority students have developed. The standardization procedures for tests such as the verbal scale of the WISC-R make it inevitable that items that might be uniquely fair to any particular minority group will be screened out in the item analysis phase since these items are unlikely to be "fair" to the majority group which, by definition, will constitute the bulk of any representative sample. Ribeiro (1980), for example, gives many examples of how WISC-R items discriminate against Azorean children. On item #12 of the Comprehension subtest ("Why is it usually better to give money to a well-known charity than to a street beggar?"), Ribeiro suggests that for a child raised within an Azorean cultural milieu, the "intelligent" response is that it is better to give money to a street beggar, since within the Azorean context giving to a beggar amounts to giving to God, whereas well-organized charities are almost nonexistent.

Thus, typical psychological assessment procedures not only fail to sample the culturally-specific skills and knowledge of the minority child, they frequently penalize children for demonstrating this knowledge.

In addition, current psychological assessment practices ignore the historical context within which the "myth of bilingual handicaps" was created. Many educators still attribute minority students' academic difficulties to their bilingualism or use of a minority language at home. Parents are frequently advised to switch to English in the home on the grounds that they jeopardize their children's academic prospects by exposing them to a language other than the school language. Although many studies carried out during the past decade totally discredit these assumptions (see Cummins, 1984, for a detailed review), they persist because they provide a convenient "explanation" for the low verbal scores often observed in assessments of minority students.

The myth that bilingualism causes academic difficulties gained credibility largely as a result of the administration of IQ tests to low socioeconomic status (SES) minority children in their weaker language (English). Comparisons were usually made with nonlingual students from middle-class backgrounds. The minority students frequently were experiencing active eradication of their language and cultural identity at school (often through physical punishment). Psychological assessment of minority students as intellectually inferior legitimizes the educational treatment by attributing students' failure to characteristics of the students themselves.

Despite the outward appearance of change, this structure still persists. Psychological assessment is still oriented towards discovery of the *student's* problem. The societal context and the classroom context are taken for granted, thereby limiting possible explanations of academic difficulties to intrinsic characteristics of the student or her cultural background. Lack of exposure to the school language is still a favored explanation for minority students' school failure. The consequent advice to parents ("Speak English") appears logical despite the likelihood that this advice will expose children to poor models of English and reduce the emotional and conceptual quality of parent-child communication. Research pointing to power relations between dominant and subordinate groups as a major contributor to minority students' academic difficulties (Cummins, 1984; Ogbu, 1978) is ignored as is research suggesting that bilingualism enhances academic functioning when a minority students' home language is encouraged to develop (Cummins, 1984).

In short, the current role relations between psychologists and minority students mirror those that helped create the myth of bilingual handicaps more than fifty years ago. Attempts to render the assessment tools used by psychologists less discriminatory will be effective only to the extent that the new tools require a change in the role relationships between assessor and assessed.[1]

THE FOCUS OF
MINORITY STUDENT ASSESSMENT

Location of the "problem" within the child is virtually inevitable when the conceptual base for the psychological assessment process is purely psycho-educational. If the psychologist's task is to discover the causes of a minority student's academic difficulties and the only tools at her disposal are psychological tests (in either L1 or L2), then it is hardly surprising that the child's difficulties will be attributed to psychological dysfunctions.

Currently, the favored diagnostic category for minority students appears to be that of "learning disability" (e.g., Ortiz and Yates, 1983; Tucker, 1980). The assumption underlying the designation of diagnostic categories (such as "learning disability") is that they can be coherently defined, reliably identified and measured, and that specific implications for remediation exist. None of these conditions are met in the case of "learning disabilities." Definitions of the construct are regarded as highly problematic by many investigators and practitioners (e.g., McIntyre, Keeton and Agard, 1980), no valid measures of the construct exist (e.g., Coles, 1978), incidence estimates in the school population vary between two percent and twenty percent (Wallace and McLoughlin, 1975), and, it has been argued, remedial pedagogy frequently violates central

[1]Feuerstein's (1979) Learning Potential Assessment Device does achieve a positive change in role relationships and is arguably the least discriminatory of current assessment procedures.

principles of language learning. As pointed out by Farnham-Diggory (1978), within the scope of the field called "learning disabilities" there are:

> ... notions of brain damage, hyperactivity, mild forms of retardation, social-emotional adjustment, language difficulties, subtle forms of deafness, perceptual problems, motor clumsiness, and, above all, reading disorders—almost the entire field of special education. (p. 2)

It is hardly surprising that the learning disability category has become a dumping ground for minority students who are failing academically. The label is regarded as an explanation. No further inquiry is necessary or desirable. The focus is on the child and the problem has been identified.

Psychologists who operate within this pattern of role definition ignore the possibility that the "learning disabilities" they have identified are pedagogically-induced. They also ignore the social pathology reflected in some patterns of dominant-subordinate group relations that gives rise to academic and identity problems for minority students. There is considerable evidence that when educators redefine the pattern of role relationships established between teachers and minority students within the classroom and between schools and minority communities, the incidence of learning difficulties is greatly reduced (Campos and Keatinge, 1983; Tizard, Schofield and Hewison, 1982). Psychologists who operate within the traditional narrow-focus model of assessment unwittingly legitimize the educational disabling of many minority students.

REDEFINING THE ROLE OF
PSYCHOLOGICAL ASSESSMENT

The alternative role definition that is required to reverse the traditional "legitimizing" function of assessment can be termed an "advocacy" or "delegitimization" role (see Mullard, 1984, for discussion of delegitimization strategies in anti-racist education). The psychologist's or special educator's task must be to "delegitimize" the traditional function of psychological assessment in the educational disabling of minority students; in other words, they must be prepared to become the advocate for the child (Cazden, 1985) in critically scrutinizing the societal and educational context within which the child has developed. This involves locating the pathology within the societal power relations between dominant and subordinate groups, in the reflection of these power relations between school and communities, and in the mental and cultural disabling of minority students that has taken and still does take place in classrooms. These conditions are the cause of the three hundred percent over-representation of Texas Hispanic students in the "learning disabled" category rather than any intrinsic processing deficit unique to Hispanic children.

Sensitivity to intrinsic processing deficits among minority children is also a legitimate function but only within the context of an "advocacy" role definition where social and educational pathologies are equally subject to critical scrutiny as contributors to minority students' academic difficulties.

Realistically, large-scale change from a "legitimization" to an "advocacy" role on the part of psychologists is unlikely. To the extent that the legitimization process functions as an integral part of a social system, it cannot change independently of that system. However, the analytic focus with respect to change presented in the present paper has been on *individual* role definitions. Thus, to the extent that individual psychologists question the assumptions underlying their role, they also challenge the social and educational structures that disable students.

An implication that follows from the present analysis is that those who train psychologists (and other educators) to use certain tools and fulfill particular roles within social systems have an ethical responsibility to simultaneously train them to question those role definitions and challenge a social system that disables minority students. Discriminatory assessment is carried out by individual people who have accepted a role definition and a socio-educational system that makes discriminatory assessment virtually inevitable.

REFERENCES

Campos, J., and Keatinge, B. *The Carpinteria Pre-School Program: Title VII Second Year Evaluation Report.* Report submitted to the Department of Health, Education, and Welfare, Office of Education, Washington, D.C., 1984.

Cazden, C. B. The ESL teacher as advocate. Plenary presentation to the TESOL Conference, New York, April 1985.

Coles, G. S. The learning disabilities test battery: Empirical and social issues. *Harvard Educational Review,* 1978, *48,* 313–340.

Cummins, J. *Bilingualism and Special Education: Issues in Assessment and Pedagogy.* San Diego, CA: College-Hill Press, 1984.

Farnham-Diggory, S. *Learning Disabilities.* Cambridge, MA: Harvard University Press, 1978.

Feuerstein, R. *The Dynamic Assessment of Retarded Performers: The Learning Potential Assessment Device, Theory, Instruments, and Techniques.* Baltimore, MD: University Park Press, 1979.

MacIntyre, R. B.; Keeton, A.; and Agard, R. *Identification of Learning Disabilities in Ontario: A Validity Study.* Toronto: Ministry of Education, Ontario, 1980.

Mehan, J.; Hertweck, A.; and Meihls, J. L. *Handicapping the Handicapped: Decision-making in Students' Educational Careers.* Palo Alto, CA: Stanford University Press, in press.

Mercer, J. R. *Labelling the Mentally Retarded.* Los Angeles, CA: University of California Press, 1973.

Mullard, C. The social dynamic of migrant groups: From progressive to transformative policy in education. Paper presented at the OECD Conference on Educational Policies and the Minority Social Groups, Paris, January 1985.

Ogbu, J. U. *Minority Education and Caste.* New York: Academic Press, 1978.

Ortiz, A. A., and Yates, J. R. Incidence of exceptionality among Hispanics: Implications for manpower planning. *NABE Journal,* 1983, 7, 41-54.

Ribeiro, J. L. Testing Portuguese immigrant children: Cultural patterns and group differences in responses to the WISC-R. In D. P. Macedo (Ed.), *Issues in Portuguese Bilingual Education.* Cambridge, MA: National Assessment and Dissemination Center for Bilingual Education, 1980.

Sanchez, G. I. Bilingualism and mental measures: A word of caution. *Journal of Applied Psychology,* 18, 765-772, 1934.

Tizard, J.; Schofield, W. N.; and Hewison, J. Collaboration between teachers and parents in assisting children's reading. *British Journal of Educational Psychology,* 1982, 52, 1-15.

Tucker, J. Ethnic proportions in classes for the learning disabled: Issues in nonbiased assessment. *Journal of Special Education,* 1980, 14, 93-105.

Wallace, G., and McLoughlin, J. *Learning Disabilities: Concepts and Characteristics.* Columbus, Ohio: Charles E. Merrill, 1975.

The general quality of bilingual research and evaluation is very poor. More and better research and improved program evaluations in bilingual education are necessary if the needs of language-minority children are to be adequately met.

KEITH BAKER and ADRIANA A. DE KANTOR
American Education

2
IDENTIFYING LANGUAGE DISORDERS IN SPANISH-SPEAKERS

Alba N. Ambert

Historically and currently, limited English proficient (LEP) children have been placed in special education programs, not because they presented clearly established learning impairments, but because they were unable to meet school expectations for functioning in English (Mercer, 1971; Tucker, 1980; Zabel, 1980; Cummins, 1984). Others have been placed in special classes due to differences in language dialect and/or cultural differences (Ambert and Melendez, 1985). Many of these children are categorized as language disordered.

Complex linguistic issues affect the diagnosis of true language disorders in Spanish-speaking children living in bilingual settings. Hispanic children whose English and Spanish varies in form and function may be misidentified as language disordered, if evaluated in English before they have fully acquired mastery of that language. Despite the critical impact appropriate evaluation of English language proficiency has on LEP children's educational placement, it is often performed improperly. An accurate appraisal of English language proficiency requires examination of diverse variables such as rate of English language acquisition, native language influence, motivation, and nature of instructional program to which the child has been exposed. Another requirement is a global language assessment which includes not only discrete items (syntax, semantics, morphology and phonology), but a child's communicative competence (the use of language for different purposes). Unless a complete assessment of English language proficiency is performed, Spanish-speaking children may appear to be fluent in English because they have acquired superficial aspects of the language. Use of English for assessment and instructional purposes with LEP children will reveal pseudo-deficits in language which are, in fact, simply gaps in the children's mastery of English at certain levels and not true language disorders at all. LEP children who do not exhibit true language impairments should not be classified as impaired solely because of limitations in English or because of cultural or dialectical differences.

In spite of these concerns, there *are* LEP children who *do* present true language disorders, and educational practitioners must meet the challenge of assessing these children appropriately. If a valid, non-discriminatory assessment is to take place, Hispanic children of limited English proficiency who appear to experience language disorders must be assessed in Spanish by clinicians with native-like fluency and who are familiar with the regional variety of the language spoken in the children's linguistic community. However, little research has been done on the linguistic characteristics of Spanish-speaking, language-disordered children living in the United States. Lack of information makes it difficult for practitioners to identify effectively Spanish-speakers with true language disorders.

Linares-Orama (1977) studied the applicability of diagnostic measures for the evaluation of syntax in preschool Spanish-speaking youngsters to determine deviancy. The study compared the performance of normal and language disordered three-year-old Puerto Rican children living in Puerto Rico. They were tested to determine whether the mean length of utterance and Lee's Developmental Sentence Scoring Procedure (1974) adapted for Spanish by Toronto (1972, 1976) were sensitive to the linguistic differences of Puerto Rican children within the three-year range. The results were positive.

Two groups of twenty-five Spanish-speaking children between the ages of six and eight were studied by Wyszewianski-Langdon (1977, 1983). One group was developing normally, the second group was composed of language disordered youngsters. A series of tests was administered to the children, in Spanish and English, in the areas of articulation of words, articulation in connected speech, auditory discrimination, sentence comprehension, sentence repetition and sentence expression. After an analysis of test results and comparisons between the groups, the author concludes that the language disordered group made more errors in both Spanish and English than the control group.

Merino (1983) compared and contrasted the language development of normal and language disordered Spanish-speaking children of limited English proficiency. A battery of tests was administered to fifty monolingual Spanish-speakers in Mexico to establish baseline data. The same battery was then administered to a group of twenty-two language disordered Spanish-speaking children in the United States. It was found that the language disordered group presented difficulties in oral production skills, but not in comprehension. Since comprehension was tested by asking the child to select one of two pictures, the results for the comprehension part of the test were less dependable, according to the author. Merino concludes that significant differences in performance exist between the language disordered and non-language disordered children on the tests.

Pragmatic criteria were compared with traditional surface structure criteria in the diagnosis of language disorders in bilingual children in a study performed by Damico, et al. (1983). Spontaneous language samples were obtained from ten Spanish/English bilingual children between six and eight years of age who had been referred for special education evaluation. The language samples were examined for normalcy following structural and pragmatic criteria. According to the authors, results of the study indicate that the two sets of criteria identified different subgroups as language impaired and that the pragmatic criteria were more effective in predicting school achievement over a seven-month period.

These studies provide valuable information on the applicability of diagnostic measures adapted for Spanish-speakers and on the importance of utilizing pragmatic criteria with traditional structural criteria in assessing language-disordered children. They also provide comparisons of language-disordered Spanish-speakers and children who are developing Spanish normally. Nevertheless, we have much to explore concerning the nature and characteristics of true language disorders in Spanish-speaking children living in the United States.

THE STUDY

The purpose of this investigation was to identify the characteristics of Spanish-speaking children living in the United States who have true language disorders and who are of limited

English proficiency. The study focused on the specific characteristics of these children's receptive and expressive language in Spanish. The influence of English on their linguistic development was considered, as well as dialectical differences in the Spanish spoken by the children involved in the study.

SUBJECTS

A group of thirty Spanish-speaking Puerto Rican children, who were both LEP and language disordered, were selected for the study. The children were between the ages of five and twelve and attended public schools in Boston, Massachusetts, and Hartford, Connecticut. As determined by the school district's administration of the Language Assessment Scales in both English and Spanish, the children were Spanish-dominant. Home language surveys indicated that the primary language of their homes was Spanish. The children were identified as language disordered by qualified bilingual speech and language pathologists who were fluent in Spanish and familiar with the regional variety of Spanish spoken by the children. The children were not mentally retarded nor did they exhibit any physical impairments. Their language difficulties were not due to English language acquisition or bilingualism and were present in their native language. All of the children were participating in bilingual education programs.

METHOD

Spanish language samples were collected on the subjects' spontaneous speech production following Bloom and Lahey's language elicitation techniques (1978). At least one hundred different utterances were collected for each child, using picture story books and a set of ten pictures to elicit language. The language samples were transcribed and analyzed for global linguistic performance, including structural analysis (phonology, morphology, syntax, and semantics) and pragmatic analysis (meaningful verbal and nonverbal interaction). In analyzing the language samples, the developmental stages of Spanish language acquisition were considered. Specifically used for this purpose was Gili-Gaya's (1974) analysis of the manner in which fifty Puerto Rican children between the ages of four and seven used language as a communication tool and for representation of ideas. An analysis of syntactic structures used by the children was also done. Also used as a comparison was Ambert's (1985) study of thirty five-year-old Spanish-speaking children in Hartford, Connecticut, whose language was developing normally.

RESULTS OF THE STUDY

The terms language disorders, language impairments and deviant language will be used interchangeably in this article to define a condition wherein a disruption in the learning of a native language occurs (Bloom and Lahey, 1978). Language processing and language production problems are evident in the language-disordered youngster (Wiig and Semel, 1976). Language-disordered children fail to make some of the linguistic generalizations necessary for appropriate use of syntactic and morphological structures (Leonard, 1972), and they appear to deviate from normal children in the frequency of usage of different grammatical structures. Menyuk (1975) confirms the breakdown of the internalization of the grammar, maintaining that language-disordered children are not simply delayed in the normal language developmental process. Although they appear to lag behind normally developing age peers on different aspects of language, it should not be assumed that these children will in time acquire language as normal speakers. In addition, children with language disorders may have difficulty not only knowing the rules of appropriate language use, but also understanding the behaviors which correspond to language use (Carrow-Woolfolk and Lynch, 1982). They lack some of the discourse, sociolinguistic and strategic competence to communicate effectively (Kessler, 1984).

True language disorders identified in this study were categorized into disorders of receptive language and disorders of expressive language. The characteristics include structural language problems as well as pragmatic language difficulties. The disorders experienced by the children in this study were evident in their general linguistic development, which in this case was in Spanish. The developmental stages of Spanish language acquisition were considered when determining whether an utterance was normal or deviant. When a five-year old, for example, overgeneralized in the formation of verb tenses (using *pusio* instead of *puso,* that is, *putted* instead of *put*) or was unable to blend the *p* and *l* sounds (saying *pato* instead of *plato* in the Spanish word for plate), it was not counted as a language deviancy. When an eight-year old produced these types of errors, however, they were considered deviant. In addition, studies on the acquisition of Spanish as a first language were used to establish deviancy. Besides the Gili-Gaya (1974) and Ambert (1985) studies, which were used extensively, the following studies were used: Montes-Giraldo's (1971) study on the chronological emergence of linguistic structures in four

21

Spanish-speaking children; Gonzalez's (1979) study of syntactical features in Spanish-speaker's language; and Belendez's (1980) study of the pattern of acquisition of the Spanish verb system in Puerto Rican children. Linguistic differences which were dialectically motivated were not considered to be deviant.

Examples of the types of errors made by children who were between the ages of eight and twelve are presented on the following pages. In these examples, the child's utterance is given followed by a slash (/) and the correct form or the intended communication. For example, pusio/puso (putted/put) means the child said *pusio* instead of *puso*. If intent is obvious, it is not indicated. Because of the syntactical differences between Spanish and English, the translations are as accurate as possible, though not always exact. Errors were evident in both the receptive and expressive domains.

RECEPTIVE LANGUAGE DISORDERS

The children in this study had intact auditory acuity, but could not process what they heard. They had difficulties establishing associations between words and meanings and in understanding questions, and had problems with auditory discrimination, word retrieval, and the ability to use gender agreement. Specific examples are as follows:

- The children were unable to associate sounds with objects or experiences. For example, some of the children could hear a word such as *lapiz* (pencil), but when asked *dame el lapiz* (give me a pencil), they would be unable to make the connection between the word and the object requested.

22

- The children could not discriminate tones, phonemes and morphemes.

tata/pata (duck)	pinto/pintor (painter)
eron/eran (were)	dio/dijo (said)
migo/amigo (friend)	dena/cadena (chain)

- The children were unable to remember words easily and often stumbled in their speech.

  Child: entonces la cosa . . . ccómo se dice esto?
  (then the thing . . . how do you say this?)

  Teacher: la cáscara (the peel)

  Child: la cáscara/y lo. la cosa que tan ¿cómo se dice?
  (the peel/and the thing that so how do you say it?)

  Teacher: la cáscara (the peel)

  Child: y entonces la cosa aquella de adentro (and then that thing there inside)

- The children experienced difficulties with gender agreement and with the use of appropriate grammatical markers for gender. (In Spanish, articles, adjectives, and pronouns carry grammatical markers which, in most cases, are either masculine or feminine.) According to Gili-Gaya (1974), by the age of four, children have consolidated the knowledge of gender which is learned through the association of each noun with the article, adjective and pronoun with which it agrees. The idea of this permanent association is tied in with the meaning of the noun and children of four years utilize gender without any problem, prior to their concept of the sexes. This is confirmed by Ambert's (1985)

23

study of five-year-olds. The following illustrates errors of gender found in the present sample (errors are underlined):

lo mama/*la* mama (the mother)
pieza es*to*/es*ta* pieza (this piece)

Question: ¿Como se sintio la mama? (How did the
mother feel?)
Child: Conten*to*/conten*ta* (happy)

- The children experienced pragmatic difficulties in their receptive language. They were unable to understand who, what, where, and why questions.

Question: ¿Quien se comio eso? (Who ate that?)
Child: sopa (soup)

Question: ¿Que rompio el nino? (What did the boy
break?
Child: Esta enferma (she's sick)

Question: ¿A donde fue Juan? (Where did Juan go?)
Child: Agriquitol (farmer)

Question: ¿Por que se mojo el lobo? (Why did the
wolf get wet?)
Child: 'tornudo (sneezed)

EXPRESSIVE LANGUAGE DISORDERS

A disorder of comprehension will necessarily affect verbal expression. Language comprehension is a skill which develops prior to full development of expressive language. Children who fail to understand do not use meaningful spoken language (Myklebust, 1954).

The language-disordered children in this study experienced varied expressive language disorders in articulation, syntax, semantics, and pragmatic language.

ARTICULATION

- The children often had difficulty pronouncing conso-nant sounds which require precise articulation, such as the *s, l, r,* and trilled *r* sounds, errors which were not consonant with their own speech community's language. For example, in the regional variety of Spanish spoken by Puerto Ricans, it is common to aspire the *s* as in *ehcuela* instead of *escuela* (school) or *casah* instead of *casas* (houses). It is also a characteristic of the Spanish spoken in Puerto Rico to transform the medial and final *r* into an *l,* as in *puelco* instead of *puerco* (pig) and *miral* instead of *mirar* (to look). These characteristics common in the Spanish spoken by Puerto Ricans should not be construed as language deviancy. They simply reflect a particular linguistic community's language usage. Errors made by the children in this study deviated from their own speech community's language patterns. For example, instead of aspirating the *s,* they would omit it entirely, and they would make inappropriate substitutions of the *r* and the trilled *r* as in the following examples:

plimo/primo (cousin)   cayo/carro (car)
canino/carino (affection)   bucala/buscarla
yompio/rompio (broke)   (look for)
                           casa/casas (houses)

- The language-disordered children also substituted, omitted, and distorted sounds:

espierto/desperto (awoke) seemdivo/se me olvido
otia/otra (another) (I forgot)
losotro/nosotros (we) guaba/guagua (bus)
ajana/regana (scold)

- They reversed the order of sounds in words:

  quichoto/chiquito (small) tabaca/estaba (was)

- and constricted words:

  ah/agua (water) cho/echo (put)
  voa/voy a (I'm going to) po/pero (but)

- They could not blend isolated sounds into meaningful segments, even though they could distinguish
  and produce such sounds as *b, l, g, r, n, s, t*:

  anco/blanco (white) motro/monstruo (monster)
  binco/brinco (jumped) pato/plato (plate)

SYNTAX

Oral syntax disordered were evident in the children studied.

- They omitted essential parts of the grammar, such as
  articles, pronouns, prepositions, the copulas *ser* and
  estar, the reflexive pronoun *se,* and conjunctions:

  casa mia es/esa casa es mia (that is my house)

  muneco muneca/un muneco y una muneca (a doll
  and a doll)

  contento/esta contento (is happy)

  un queso/con un queso (with a cheese)

26

el fue/el se fue (he left)

mia muñeca/la muñeca es mia (the doll is mine)

- They used incorrect word order:

olvidó eso Luis/A Luis se le olvidó eso (Luis forgot that)

jirafa quiere él/él quiere la jirafa (he wants the giraffe)

Charlie Brown yo lo vi/yo vi a Charlie Brown (I saw Charlie Brown)

- They substituted articles, pronouns and other grammatical structures with the *schwa* sound, which is written with the symbol Ə and pronounced as the *e* in roses.

¿Ə pegaron eso? ¿Quiénes pegaron eso? (Who pasted that?)

Ə vuela/eso vuela (that flies)

Ə pongo 'torio Luis/lo pongo en el escritorio de Luis (I put it in Luis' desk)

Ə guardo hago esta/lo guardo y hago esta (I'll save it and do this one)

- They exhibited lack of noun-verb and article-noun agreement.

el sapo no puedan hablar /los sapos no puedan hablar (frogs cannot talk)

lo mamá/la mamá (the mother)

se cayó/se cayeron (they fell)

- They omitted plural endings.

    dos árbol/dos árboles (two trees)

    se montaron solo/se montaron solos (they got on alone)

    tumbó flor/tumbó las flores (knocked down the flowers)

- They confused verb tenses.

    pónelo/pónlos (put them)
    viste/vi (I saw)
    hació/hizo (made)
    cayó las flores/las flores se cayeron (the flowers fell)

- Omission of the auxiliary *estar* in the present progressive form was common.

    corriendo/está corriendo (is running)
    jugando/está jugando (is playing)

SEMANTICS

The children in this study demonstrated difficulties with word meanings:

- They used inappropriate verbal labels for common objects, actions, and persons.

    música/película (music/film)
    radio/teléfono (radio/telephone)
    hablar/sonreir (talk/smile)
    niño/conejito (boy/bunny)

- They used circumlocution when they could not retrieve words.

papel que se usa pa'buscar en la tierra/mapa
(paper that's used to look in the ground/map

una traba que se mece/columpio
(a board that sways/swing)

la luz que se cambia pa' cororá/semáforo
(the light that changes to red/traffic light

no hace frío y hace calor/verano
(it's not cold and it's hot/summer)

- In the pragmatic area of expressive language disorders, the children had difficulties retelling stories or narrating personal experiences. They frequently depended on gestures and pointing to be understood.

| Question: | ¿Si? cQue te paso? Cuentame. (Really? What happened? Tell me.) |
| Child: | No response. |

| Question: | ¿A donde fue Juan? (Where did Juan go?) |
| Child: | a la . . . ccomo se dice eso? (to the . . . how do you say that?) |

| Question: | ¿Te gustaba ordeñar la cabra? (Did you like to milk the goat?) |
| Child: | Ajá.y entonces y pue cuando la cabla. (Aha.and then and so when the goat.) |

| Question: | ¿Cómo se llaman tus amigos? (What are your friends' names?) |
| Child: | Yo no sé. (I don't know) |

- The children had difficulty classifying events with verbal labels and organizing words in appropriate sentences.

y había soda por dentro que había una tiendita/
había una tiendita que tenía soda
(there was a store which had soda)

lo puso así [gestures] a que lo puso así y lo hizo bien
(he put it like this [gestures] put it like this and did
   well)

- They were unable to correct grammatical errors in
  sentence construction in many instances.

y la señora.am.le hizo a lo carro que parena
y la señora hizo que los carros pararan
(the lady made the cars stop)

todo el lado/todos los lados
(on all sides)

In addition to the linguistic deviations described, the use of idiomatic expressions was rare in the children studied, as was the use of adjectives, adverbs, possessive articles other than *mi* or *mío,* the use of the present progressive, prepositions, the reflexive *se,* the auxiliaries *ser* and *estar,* copulas *ser* and *estar,* and the periphrastic future (ir a + infinitive).

Although the Spanish-speaking language-disordered children described in this study were participating in English-as-a-Second Language (ESL) programs, the English language influence on their acquisition of Spanish was minimal. The only discernible English influence evident was in vocabulary. They used words such as Istel/Easter, estim/steam, matre/mattress, fensa/fence, listi/lipstick, hi and hall. It is common for Spanish-speakers living in the United States to use these English terms with a Spanish pronunciation and their use is not indicative of a language disorder.

30

CONCLUSION

Hispanic children of limited English proficiency have been frequently misidentified as language disordered. This situation occurs when they are assessed in English, a language they do not master, or when they are observed in an all-English instructional program where their performance is judged against the performance of native speakers of the English language. Misidentification also occurs when Hispanic LEP children are assessed in Spanish by assessors who are not fluent in Spanish and/or not familiar with the regional variety of Spanish spoken by the child. Educational practitioners must exercise much caution and ascertain that the LEP children's assessments are performed in the native language by qualified bilingual professionals according to legal requirements and sound educational practices.

Since there *are* instances in which Hispanic LEP children experience linguistic difficulties in the native language due to a language impairment, it is essential that practitioners recognize the nature and characteristics of language impairments in Spanish-speaking children.

The purpose of the present study was to describe the characteristics of Spanish-speaking children with true language disorders to assist educators in appropriately identifying LEP Hispanic children who would benefit from a language intervention program.

It was found that the language of language disordered Hispanic children of limited-English proficiency included in this study deviated from the language of Spanish-speaking children acquiring language normally. The children presented structural difficulties as well as pragmatic problems. The children studied were living in a bilingual setting, yet the impact of English on their language development was minimal.

REFERENCES

Ambert, A. N. "Language enriched Spanish-speaking children." Massachusetts Institute of Technology, Cambridge, Massachusetts, 1985 (to be published).

Ambert, A. N. "The identification of LEP children with special needs." *Bilingual Journal,* 1982, 6:17-22.

Ambert, A. N., and Melendez, S. E. *Bilingual Education: A Sourcebook.* New York: Garland Publishing, 1985.

Belendez, P. Repetitions and the Acquisition of the Spanish Verb System. Unpublished doctoral dissertation, Harvard University Graduate School of Education, 1980.

Bloom, L., and Lahey, M. *Language Development and Language Disorders.* New York: Wiley, 1978.

Carrow-Woolfolk, E., and Lynch, J. I. *An Integrative Approach to Language Disorders in Children.* Grune & Stratton, 1982.

Cummins, J. *Bilingualism and Special Education: Issues in Assessment and Pedagogy.* Avon, England: Multilingual Matters, 1984.

Damico, J. S.; Oller, J. W.; and Storey, M. E. "The diagnosis of language disorders in bilingual children: Surface-oriented and pragmatic criteria." *Journal of Speech and Hearing Disorders,* 1973, 46:385-394.

Gili-Gaya, S. *Estudios de lenguaje infantil.* Barcelona, Spain: Vox Bibliograf, 1974.

Gonzalez, G. *The Acquisition of Spanish Grammar by Native Spanish-Speaking Children.* Rossly, VA: National Clearinghouse for Bilingual Education, 979.

Kessler, C. "Language acquisition in bilingual children." In Miller, N. (Ed.), *Bilingualism and Language Disability.* San Diego, CA: College Hill Press, 1984.

Lee, L. *Developmental Sentence Analysis.* Evanston, IL: Northwestern University Press, 1974.

Leonard, L. B. "What is deviant language?" *Journal of Speech and Hearing Disorders,* 1972, 37:427-446.

Linares-Orama, N. "Evaluation of syntax in three-year-old Spanish-speaking Puerto Rican children." *Journal of Speech and Hearing Research,* 1977, 20:350-357.

Menyuk, P. "Children with language problems: What's the problem?" In Dato, D. P. (Ed.), *Georgetown University Roundtable on Languages and Linguistics*. Washington, D.C.: Georgetown University Press, 1975.

Mercer, J. R. "Institutionalized anglocentrism: Labeling mental retardates in ten schools." In Orleans, P., and Russel, W. (Eds.), *Race, Change and Urban Society.* Los Angeles, CA: Sage Publications, 971.

Merino, B. J. "Language development in normal and language handicapped Spanish-speaking children.: *Hispanic Journal of Behavioral Sciences,* 1983, 5:379-400.

Montes-Giraldo, J. J. "Acerca de la apropiacion por el nino del sistema fonologico espanol." *Thesaurus,* 1971, 26:322-346.

Myklebust, H. *Auditory Disorders in Children: A Manual for Differential Diagnosis.* New York: Grune & Stratton, 1954.

Toronto, A. A Developmental Spanish Language Analysis Procedure for Spanish-speaking Children. Unpublished doctoral dissertation, Northwestern University, 1972.

Toronto, A. "Developmental assessment of Spanish grammar." *Journal of Speech and Hearing Disorders,* 1976, 41:150-171.

Tucker, J. A. "Ethnic proportions in classes for the learning disabled: Issues in nonbiased assessment." *Journal of Special Education,* 1980, 14:93-105.

Wiig, E. H., and Semel, E. M. *Language Disabilities in Children and Adolescents.* Columbus, Ohio: Merrill, 1976.

Wyszewianski-Langdon, H. Determining a Language Disorder in a Bilingual Spanish-English Population. Unpublished doctoral dissertation, Boston University, 1977.

Wyszewianski-Langdon, H. "Assessment and intervention strategies for the bilingual language disordered student." *Exceptional Children,* 1983, 50:37-46.

Zabel, R. H. "Identification and Referral Procedures: Linguistic and Cultural Considerations." Paper presented at the Bilingual Special Education Conference, Evanston, Illinois, National College of Education, May, 1980.

With the possible exception of desegregation, no subject has aroused the passion that characterizes debate over how schools should go about educating students with limited English proficiency.

EDWARD B. FISKE
The New York Times

3

REDUCING INAPPROPRIATE REFERRALS OF LANGUAGE MINORITY STUDENTS IN SPECIAL EDUCATION

Alba A. Ortiz and Elba Maldonado-Colon

The Education for All Handicapped Children Act of 1975, Public Law 94-142, requires that assurances be provided that a child's problems are not due to differences of language, culture, socioeconomic status, or to not having had opportunities to learn. Preliminary findings of a study conducted under the auspices of the University of Texas at Austin Handicapped Minority Research Institute on Language Proficiency indicate that such assurances are routinely provided for virtually all limited English proficient (LEP) students. However, when student records are examined, it is difficult to determine what data, if any, were deliberated to provide this certification. This procedural safeguard, then, is reduced to simple compliance with a bureaucratic requirement and little consideration is given to the significance of this action by placement committees. The long-term, and potentially negative, effects of special education placement on a student's social, academic, and vocational future warrants a critical look at the effectiveness of referral, assessment, and placement procedures for language minority students.

Ortiz and Yates (1983, 1984) suggest that normal, but underachieving, language minority students are dramatically over-represented in programs for the learning disabled. These inappropriate placements are an artifact of the referral process; children are referred to special education on the basis of behaviors which do not fit the expectations of educators and are placed, not because they require special education services, but because placement committees erroneously interpret linguistic, cultural, economic or other background characteristics as deviant. While one could argue that language minority students profit from the individualized instruction provided by specially trained teachers, the placement of underachieving (as opposed to handicapped) students in special education decreases the effectiveness of appraisal and instructional personnel available to serve the handicapped.

The key to reducing inappropriate special education placements is to reduce inappropriate referrals. Educators must be made aware that some behaviors, while they do not conform to the norms or expectations of members of the majority society, are normal given an individual's reference or social group and his/her prior experiences. Such behaviors are better characterized as *differences,* rather than as deficits or handicapping conditions. Accommodating individual differences to increase the likelihood of school success is, first and foremost, the responsibility of regular educators, not of special education personnel.

PROBLEM BEHAVIORS: ALTERNATIVE EXPLANATIONS

Table 1 presents a student behavior checklist similar to those used by school districts to help teachers and others support their referrals to special education. These checklists are intended

to capture problem behaviors which the
warrant special education intervention. H(
ior characteristics on the checklist marked by
just as likely to reflect *normal* behavior for some stud
the following sections, two examples of normal, but different
behavior are used to illustrate this point.

Language

Behaviors directly or indirectly related to linguistic proficiency constitute the most frequent reason for referral of language minority students (Carpenter, 1983; Garcia, 1984; Maldonado-Colon, 1984; Ortiz and Yates, 1983; Shepard and Smith, 1981). The research literature documents that many of the behaviors considered problematic by teachers are, in reality, characteristic of students who are in the process of normal second language acquisition. This can be seen by comparing the behaviors in Table 1, those marked with one asterisk (*), with the following descriptors of *normal* second language acquirers:

1. Limited comprehension and production of the second language (Dulay, Burt and Krashen, 1982);

2. Errors in production of the phonemes of the second language or the use of other structures or words to replace those sounds the child is either unable to produce or which cause confusion (Barkin, 1982; Celce-Murcia, 1978);

3. Temporary competition between the two languages, commonly referred to as the interlingual stage (Dulay, Burt and Krashen, 1982; Selinker, 1972);

4. Inappropriate syntax and grammar (Saville-Troike, 1976);

TABLE 1
Student Behavior Checklist

Attention/Order	Personal/Emotional	Interpersonal/Social	Adult Relations/Authority	School Adaptation	Language
*Short attention span	Sad/Unhappy	Has few friends	Talks back to adults	Disrupts other students	Speaks excessively
*Distractable	*Nervous/Anxious	Verbally aggressive	Intimidated by authority	Speaks out of turn	*Speaks infrequently
Talks excessively	*Shy/Timid	**Denies responsibility for actions	Overly anxious to please	**Does not complete assignments	*Uses gestures
*Daydreams	Short tempered				*Speaks in single words or phrases
Unable to wait turn	*Poor self-confidence	Instigates misbehaviors in others	**Passively uncooperative	**Cannot work independently	*Refuses to answer questions
Loud and noisy	Extreme mood changes				
Constant need for stimulation	Cries easily	**Easily influenced	Distrustful of adults	Copies other's work	*Does not volunteer information
Hyperactive	Unusual mannerisms or habits	Bossy	Refuses to accept limits	**Exerts little effort	
**Demands immediate gratification	*Fearful	**Demands attention	**Defiant	**Lacks interest/apathetic	*Comments inappropriately
*Disorganized	Easily excitable	Inconsiderate	Ambivalent toward adults	Frequently tardy or absent	*Poor recall
		Selfish			

*Unable to stay on task	Inappropriate emotional responses	Lies	Uses profanity	**Gives up easily	*Poor comprehension
*Appears confused	Immature	Steals	**Clings to adults	**Cannot manage time	*Poor vocabulary
	Toileting problems	Jealous	**Overly dependent	**Lacks drive	*Difficulty sequencing ideas
	*Difficulty in adjusting to new situations	Can't keep hands to self	**Seeks constant praise	**Disorganized	*Difficulty sequencing events
	Cruel	Manipulates others	Rebellious	**Cannot plan	*Unable to tell or retell stories
	Uncooperative	Suspicious	**Needs teacher direction and feedback	**Unable to tolerate change	*Confuses similar sounding words
	Loses control	*Cannot handle criticism		**Sporadic academic performance	*Poor pronunciation
	Overreacts	**Avoids competition		Makes excuses	*Poor syntax/grammar
		Prefers to be alone		Destructive	
		Physically aggressive		**Does not initiate	
				Needs reminding	

*Normal behavior characteristics – often referred because different from expectations.

**Behavior characteristics frequently associated with learning disabilities.

5. Limited or inappropriate use of lexicon (Saville-Troike, 1976);

6. Code-switching, switching from one language to another (Trudgill, 1976), used as an ethnic or social marker or as a transition tool as the child acquires the second language (Garcia, Maez & Gonzalez, n.d.; Penalosa, 1980), or resulting from being forced to speak a language before having adequate control (Krashen, 1981);

7. Gradual or partial loss of the first or the second language (Lambert and Freedman, 1982; Watson and Omark, 1982).

That the preceding behaviors are included on behavior problem checklists reflects confusion about what distinguishes linguistic differences from language or learning disabilities. It is not surprising, then, that referral and placement committees may disregard the fact that the child is a second language learner; further, the appropriateness of their decision is open to question given a lack of understanding of language proficiency, bilingualism, and of how limited English proficient students acquire the English language (Cummins, 1981, 1984; Maldonado-Colon, 1985; Shepard and Smith, 1981).

The case of the code-switcher illustrates a common misconception about native language acquisition. When Hispanic children who code-switch are tested in both English and in Spanish, it is not unusual for them to obtain low scores in both languages. Because of their poor performance, these children are considered to be language disordered or delayed and are described as being "alingual," without language, or "semilingual," limited in both languages. This interpretation disregards the fact that some children are exposed to mixed language models in their home and community; for these children, code-switching is not a mixture of two separate language systems but, rather, constitutes a unique communication system, with its own rules and restrictions. This implies that high performance in either language alone is not necessarily to be expected and that the child should not be penalized for failure to demonstrate such. Evaluations which take this into account usually point to programs for language development and enrichment in mainstream settings, not to remedial programs in special education.

There is also a lack of understanding of the relationship between the native language and the second language (Cummins, 1981). The research literature is rather clear that the child's proficiency in English is dependent upon his/her level of native language proficiency. It is unfortunate that native language development is interrupted for those students who are not eligible to participate in bilingual education programs. These students receive English-only instruction in regular classroom settings and the subsequent lack of rich native language stimulation diminishes the potential for high levels of proficiency in the second language (Cummins, 1981; Krashen, 1981; Skutnabb-Kangas, 1980). This exclusive emphasis on English instruction not only interferes with a natural developmental sequence, but also triggers the possibility of native language loss (Lambert and Freedman, 1982). Language loss further limits academic potential because of its negative effects on second language acquisition (Krashen, 1981; Skutnabb-Kangas, 1980).

A word of caution is necessary in the case of bilingual children who seem to have adequate English skills. Many students manage to rapidly acquire the surface structures of English and impress professionals as having the linguistic abilities necessary to handle the complex context-reduced language which is used by teachers and found in textbooks and other instructional materials. When these students begin to experience achievement difficulties, a referral to special education is likely to follow. Lack of English proficiency is ruled out as a possible cause of the problem because the child appears to have no difficulty understanding or communicating with teachers or peers. These students, while they demonstrate good interpersonal communication skills, need more time to obtain academic language proficiency required for schooling (Cummins, 1981; 1984). Unless sufficient time is afforded, the possibility of school failure will be exacerbated.

It is the role of appraisal personnel to conduct evaluations which will ascertain whether a child's problem can be attributed to a handicapping condition, or to the fact that he/she is in the process of learning English. This distinction is critical and merits careful deliberation since appropriate and effective intervention depends on the ability of professionals to tell the difference.

Learned Helplessness.

There are students who continuously meet with academic failure because of incompatibilities between the way they learn and the way teachers teach. Various terms have been used to discuss behaviors of these students, including internal versus external locus of control (Vasquez, 1975); learned helplessness (Henderson, 1980); field independence versus field sensitivity (Ramirez and Castaneda, 1974); and cultural deprivation

(Feuerstein, 1980). These authors suggest that for a variety of reasons, including socioeconomic level or minority status, certain students exhibit behaviors which predispose them to school failure.

For example, Vasquez (1975) submits that students with an external locus of control will experience achievement difficulties. Locus of control is a term which describes to whom or what an individual attributes his successes or failures. A person with an internal locus of control credits accomplishments to his/her own skills, abilities, or efforts; an external person believes outcomes are controlled by powerful others (e.g., teachers) or are the result of luck, chance, or fate. Vasquez enumerates characteristics common to students with an external locus of control, including the following:

1. Self-reliance
   a. Prefers to work in groups
   b. Cannot work independently
   c. Seeks teacher direction and feedback

2. Achievement Motivation
   a. Does not set goals
   b. Does not know how to plan
   c. Cannot break tasks down into component parts

3. Expectancy of Success and Reaction to Reinforcement
   a. Does not see cause-effect relationships
   b. Cannot anticipate how things will work out

     c. Reacts in similar ways to success and failure

     d. Appears to lack motivation

4. Intensity of Effort

     a. Does not know how to change own behavior to influence outcomes

     b. Does not generalize

     c. Does not apply prior learning to new tasks

5. Performance Under Skill Conditions

     a. Does not like competition

     b. Does not analyze difficulty of tasks

     c. Frustrates easily

     d. Does not complete assignments

Many of the behaviors which Vasquez attributes to differences in cognitive or learning style are also found on the student behavior checklist in Table 1. As a matter of fact, the behaviors marked by two asterisks (**) closely parallel behaviors which are frequently associated with learning disabilities. It is critical, then, that teachers be aware that in some instances these behaviors are normal, but reflect cultural or socioeconomic status differences; in other instances, they indeed suggest a handicapping condition.

DOCUMENTING PRIOR INTERVENTIONS

The key to distinguishing differences from handicapping conditions is the careful documentation of prior interventions. For example, external students are unlikely to analyze their performance or feedback to determine how to change their behavior to become more successful in the school system. Feuerstein (as cited in Chance, 1981) suggests that they fail to recognize that their own intellectual efforts may contribute to the solution of a problem and, instead, see themselves as passive recipients of information. Their difficulties may be the result of a lack of mediated learning experiences (MLE).

The MLE is a process by which someone, usually an adult, assists the child in interpreting and organizing stimuli in the direction of a specific goal or outcome. Stopping at a red light is a *direct* experience; having an adult point out that "red" means "stop" is a *mediated* learning experience. Two few mediated experiences can result in poor thinking skills which, in turn, reduces the individual's ability to learn from direct experiences. Neither remedial efforts aimed at providing a stimulating environment nor emphasis on traditional academics will be effective in overcoming cognitive deficiencies. Instead, what is called for is that someone mediate learning experiences and frame the stimuli to provide insight into the thinking process. Instructional intervention should be aimed at teaching *how* solutions are derived and *how* facts are acquired. In essence, the student must be taught how to learn if he/she is to be expected to conform to expectations of school programs and personnel.

If the external child is exposed to learning strategies, and instruction is linguistically and culturally relevant, improved performance would suggest that achievement difficulties could be attributed to *differences* associated with cognitive or learning style. However, if the student continues to experience difficulty, even after the teacher has adapted the instructional environment to accommodate learning style, then a referral to special education would be appropriate. The teacher will be able to provide careful documentation which shows not only that curricula and instruction were adapted, but that these adaptations reflect an understanding of, and are consistent with, unique student characteristics. Only in this way can decision-making committees be more confident that problems are not the result of differences of language, culture, socioeconomic status, lifestyle, or to not having had opportunities to learn.

REFERENCES

Barkin, F. (1980). *Southwest Area Language and Linguistics Workshop.* Tempe, AZ: Arizona State University.

Carpenter, L. (1983). *Communication Disorders in Limited- and Non-English Proficient Children.* Los Alamitos, CA: National Center for Bilingual Research.

Celce-Murcia, M. (1978). The simultaneous acquisition of English and French in a two-year-old child. In E. M. Hatch (Ed.), *Second Language Acquisition* (pp. 38-53). Rowley, MA: Newbury House.

Chance, P. (1981). The remedial thinker. *Psychology Today, 16,* 63-73.

Cummins, J. (1981). The role of primary language development in promoting education success for language minority students. In *Schooling and Language Minority Students: A Theoretical Framework* (p. 3-49). Los Angeles, CA: California State University.

Cummins, J. (1984). *Bilingualism and Special Education: Issues in Assessment and Pedagogy.* Clevedon, Avon: Multilingual Matters.

Dulay, H.; Burt, M.; & Krashen, S. (1982). *Language Two.* New York: Oxford University Press.

Feuerstein, R. (1980). *Instrumental Enrichment: An Intervention Program for Cognitive Modifiability.* Baltimore, MD: University Park Press.

Garcia, S. B. (1984). Effects of student characteristics, school program and organization on decision-making for the placement of Hispanic students in classes for the learning disabled. Unpublished doctoral dissertation. The University of Texas at Austin.

Garcia, M.; Maez, L.; & Gonzalez, G. (nd). *A National Study of Spanish English Bilingualism Among Young Hispanic Children of the United States.* Los Angeles, CA: National Dissemination and Assessment Center.

Krashen, S. D. (1981). Bilingual education and second language acquisition theory. In *Schooling and Language Minority Students: A Theoretical Framework* (pp. 51-79). Los Angeles, CA: California State University.

Lambert, R. D., & Freedman, B. F. (Eds.) (1982). *The Loss of Language Skills.* Rowley, MA: Newbury House.

Maldonado-Colon, E. (1984). *Profiles of Hispanic Students Placed in Speech, Hearing and Language Programs in a Selected School District in Texas.* Doctoral dissertation. University of Massachusetts. Ann Arbor, MI: University of Microfilms International (No. 84-10309).

Maldonado-Colon, E. (1985). *The Role of Language Assessment Data in Diagnosis and Intervention for Linguistically/Culturally Different Students.* Reston, VA: ERIC Clearinghouse on Handicapped and Gifted Children.

Ortiz, A.; & Yates, J. R. (1983). Incidence of exceptionality among Hispanics: Implications for manpower planning. *NABE JOURNAL,* 7(3), 41-53.

Ortiz, A. A.; & Yates, J. R. (1984). Linguistically and culturally diverse handicapped students. In R. Podemski, D. Price, T. Smith, and G. Marsh, II (Eds.), *Comprehensive Administration of Special Education* (pp. 114-141). Rockville, MD: Aspen Systems.

Penalosa, F. (1980). *Chicano Scoiolinguistics: A Brief Introduction.* Rowley, MA: Newbury House.

Saville-Troike, M. (1973). *Bilingual Children: A Resource Document.* Arlington, VA: Center for Applied Linguistics.

Selinker, L. (1972). Interlanguage. *International Review of Applied Linguistics, 10,* 209-231.

Shepard, L.; & Smith, M. L. (1981). *Evaluation of the Identification of Perceptual-communicative disorders in Colorado (Final Report).* Boulder, CO: Laboratory of Educational Research.

Skutnabb-Kangas, T. (1980). *Language in the Process of Cultural Assimilation and Structural Incorporation of Linguistic Minorities.* Rosslyn, VA: National Clearinghouse for Bilingual Education.

Trudgill, P. (1976). *Sociolinguistics: An Introduction.* New York: Penguin Books.

Vasquez, J. (1975). Locus of control, social class and learning. In *School Desegregation and Cultural Pluralism: Perspectives in Progress.* San Francisco, CA: Service, Training, and Research in Desegregated Education, Far West Laboratory for Educational Research & Development.

Bilingual education has effectively opened the schoolhouse door to hundreds of thousands of parents who historically have been locked out.

JAMES J. LYONS, legislative counsel
National Association for Bilingual Education

4

THE PARENT FACTOR IN TEACHING LANGUAGE SKILLS TO LIMITED ENGLISH PROFICIENT LEARNING DISABLED STUDENTS

Angela Carrasquillo

Professionals in the field of special education and bilingual education have become aware of the need to provide an appropriate education for language minority students with special needs. However, adequate information regarding appropriate identification, placement, and programming procedures that best benefit these students is not abundant. This limited research base makes it difficult to develop educational procedures that most benefit these students. In order to bridge these gaps, schools must make use of whatever resources are available to provide adequate and effective instruction to language minority students. Of these resources, the most important and useful one to schools is parents. Parents of special education students are primary helpers, teachers, reinforcers and decision-makers for their children. It is important that the school staff responsible for the students' instructional component (especially the principal and the classroom teacher) stay in close contact with parents. This article will highlight emerging issues and strategies concerning how parents and teachers can build a mutually supportive instructional relationship to help learning disabled limited English proficient (LEP) students to acquire and further develop language skills.

The definition of learning disabilities is taken from the Handicapped Children's Act (PL 94-142) which defines a learning disability as "a disorder in one or more of the basic psychological processes involved in understanding or in using language, spoken or written, which may manifest itself in an imperfect ability to listen, think, speak, read, write, spell or to do mathematical calculations" (Federal Register, 1982, pp. 338-45). The concept of language skills discussed in this article is a broad one which includes concept development, listening, speaking, reading and writing. Both bilingual education and special education program instructional requirements are based on the notion that instructional services provided must take into account the students' unique characteristics. In special education classes, parents should be consulted at the assessment and instructional phase. Parents have the legal right to participate in the development of their child's individualized educational program (IEP). Schools should take advantage of the opportunity provided in PL 94-142 and work as closely as possible with the limited English proficient disabled student.

THE ACQUISITION OF LANGUAGE AND THE LEARNING DISABLED LEP STUDENT

The normal development of language is dependent upon a combination of factors. Initially, in order for a child to acquire a language system, the child must possess an intact nervous and muscular system that permits understanding and the use of the phonological, morphological, syntactical and semantic components of language. A child learns language by actively exploring meanings in the context of interaction with others. The focus of this interaction is constantly on the meaning or intentions being conveyed by the participants rather than on the forms of the language itself. Donaldson (1978) and MacNamara (1966) have pointed out that the meanings of words can only be inferred by the young child on the basis of prior understanding of the meaning of the concrete and social situation in which the words are embedded. A normal child learns almost instinctively to select the right word, the right response and the right gesture to fit the situation. Children do not learn language first and then use it; rather, they learn language at the same time as they are using the language to learn other things. For most children, development of thought and spoken language abilities occur with remarkable speed and ease. As normal children grow older, they demonstrate increasingly complex behaviors that indicate the acquisition of both receptive and expressive language usage.

A significant number of students enrolled in special education classes are labeled as "learning disabled students." Although this term is vague and covers a wide variety of learning and behavioral difficulties, Halløahan and Cruickshank (1973) have found that many of the children enrolled in learning disability classes show some type of language disorder. Myklebust (1965) states that the disability may occur at the level of perception, imagery, symbolization or deconceptualization in describing the characteristics of students with learning disabilities. Gearheart (1985) has identified three of those characteristics as being directly language related. He says:

> *Delayed spoken language development.* This may include characteristics such as limited vocabulary, immature vocabulary, unusually large number of grammatical errors, diffi-

culty in relating ideas in logical sequence and regular "groping" for words.

Inability to follow class discussions. This may include inability to understand the flow of thought while other students are discussing class topics.

Perceptual disorders. This may include disorders of visual, auditory, tactual or kinesthetic perception. The child with visual-perceptual problems may not be able to copy letters correctly or to perceive the difference between a hexagon or an octagon. (pp. 16-17)

There are a large group of limited English proficient students enrolled in special education classes due to the confusion of identifying non-English speakers as language disabled students. Some of the above characteristics can be applied to LEP students and, if appropriate testing and screening are not done, many of these students showing one of these characteristics due to language deficiencies or differences might be placed in learning disabled classes. The crucial issue is to differentiate between language differences and language disorders. Historically, LEP students who presented behavioral or instructional difficulties for the classroom teacher were referred and placed in special education classes. The child's language and background differences were interpreted as inadequate linguistic skills, unresponsiveness to learning and low achievement (Baca and Cervantes, 1984). It is imperative that when schools receive LEP students, the screening, assessment and placement of students is not done prematurely. One must not confuse temporary deficiencies due to unfamiliarity with the English language with language disorders.

The primary purpose of schooling for LEP students is not the mere acquisition of English, but should include the acquisition and development of cognitive skills (Baca and Cervantes, 1984). Development of cognitive academic skills includes the acquisition of skills such as reading, writing, organizing and development of concept and abstract ideas. When meaningful opportunities are provided for comprehensible language input along with positive motivation to learn English, language minority students will acquire the basic communicative skills (Cummins, 1985; Krashen, 1982). Limited English disabled students will show profound language disabilities in their native language in more than one of the already discussed categories. When learning English, severe language deficiencies are also observed in the creative use of language and in the meaningful language interactions rather than in grammatical or form errors.

THE PARENT AS A PARTICIPANT

Much has been said about the need for parent involvement. Parents play a key role in their children's physical, emotional, social, cognitive and academic development. For linguistically and culturally different students it is almost impossible to develop a curriculum that is continuous and effective for each. Thus, there is a need to develop support systems that contribute to the students' continuous development. The primary support system for the school and the students are the parents. Anderson and Safar (1967) have indicated that parent involvement in school activities is determined, among other factors, by the extent of participation allowed by the school's decision-making unit. Although special education legislation requires parent participation, in many instances this participation is minimal.

Families may be disorganized, unstable, restrictive, non-verbal, or organized, stable, enriching, verbal and bilingual (Baca and Cervantes). This is why schools must develop strategies to work with all parents. The question that always arises is what the school's role should be with respect to parent participation. Is it to train the parents, to educate them, to use them in the classroom, or to use them at home as reinforcers? A possible answer would be that the school should have a role in all of the above. However, this is too much for most schools to realistically accomplish, as each of the mentioned programs is very expensive. The participation of parents who themselves are of limited English proficiency is even more difficult due to the fact that these parents cannot integrate adequately with the school, especially since they do not understand the culture and language of the school. Also, a high percentage of these parents do not have the necessary academic skills to be teacher aides, even in their native language. Parents of LEP students can be used most effectively as instructional reinforcers of school work, especially in the areas of language and cognitive development. Once parents see themselves as reinforcers of the school work, they become more involved as school monitors, school advocates, and school translators.

PARENTS AS HOME REINFORCERS
OF LANGUAGE SKILLS DEVELOPMENT

There are several ways in which parents with some guidance and orientation can help in the development of language skills. Parents can help at home by reinforcing or expanding skills already taught at school and by providing social and emotional support to learning disabled students. The legal requirement that parents must participate in the development of the student IEP might provide an opportunity to develop a plan for a parent school reinforcement program. This program can be a whole school program or an individual classroom program. Either way, the principal, the teacher, the parent and the student have to agree on the need for such a program. Meetings have to be organized to explain the philosophy of the program, the programmatic steps and the instructional responsibilities of each member of the team. Since the parents of linguistically minority students represent a variety of language and academic backgrounds, and since not all the students reflect the same language disabilities, all parents cannot be required to accomplish the same tasks. The following case studies serve to demonstrate specific examples of the suggested instructional strategies for parents in the role of school work reinforcers.

Case #1

Mrs. Melendez is a single parent. She came from Santo Domingo five years ago. She reads and writes Spanish fairly well. She understands some English, but it is difficult for her to maintain a conversation in English. She has three children in school. Carlos is ten years old and is enrolled in a special education class. Marianela is in the second grade. Efrain is in the first grade. When Mrs. Melendez was invited to the school to discuss Carlos' IEP with the teacher, Mrs. Melendez informed the teacher, among other things, that Carlos' home speaking activities were minimal.

DISCUSSION

Mrs. Melendez represents many of the parents of language minority students. In normal circumstances, Mrs. Melendez will not be able to help her children, especially Carlos, since she does not have the academic background to know what to teach and where to start. However, it is necessary that the school finds ways to help Mrs. Melendez reinforce what the school is teaching Carlos. Although she does not have a satisfactory understanding of English, she can provide reinforcement in cognitive areas in English as well as in the native language. It is assumed that Carlos is attending a bilingual program with a well developed English as a second language component. When the instructional team meets with Mrs. Melendez to inform her of her son's individual educational program and the home reinforcement program, the following instructional strategies should be mentioned:

1. Since Mrs. Melendez informed the teacher that Carlos' speaking activities at home were minimal, the team should encourage Mrs. Melendez to communicate with her son in his native language in order to motivate her son to see the need to communicate. As Cummins (1985) has said, children do not solely acquire language by imitating adult models who correct errors and reinforce correct forms, but through actively participating and exploring meanings or intentions being conveyed by the participants (p. 225). However, Mrs. Melendez by herself probably will not provide meaningful interaction experiences for Carlos. The teacher should provide Mrs. Melendez with weekly language interaction exercises, if possible in both languages.

Exercises might include: native language short stories, folklore/cultural anecdotes, and games with the specific intention of creative vocabulary development.

2. Mrs. Melendez should not be forced to switch to English in order to increase exposure to English and eliminate language difficulties. Cummins and Ortiz (1985) have pointed out that there is no direct relationship between exposure to the majority language and achievement in that language. Another misconception is that handicapped children who are limited English proficient will have difficulty developing language skills and should be given as much time as possible to master the English language. Mrs. Melendez instead needs language activities to develop activities in which the strong promotion of the native language's conceptual skills will be effective in providing a basis for the acquisition of English oral language and literacy skills for herself and her son.

Case #2

Mr. and Mrs. Bordeaux came from Haiti four years ago. Mr. Bordeaux is a supervisor in a department store, while Mrs. Bordeaux stays at home and takes care of their two sons. Both of them were placed in special education classes for learning disabled students. While in Haiti, Mr. and Mrs. Bordeaux spoke Creole at home and learned to read and write French in school. Both children demonstrate some knowledge of French and Creole. At their arrival in the United States, both children were placed in bilingual classes— French/English. Six months later, after the teacher referral and the educational evaluation assessment, both children were placed in special education classes. When discussing the IEP, Mr. and Mrs. Bordeaux informed the teacher that they noticed that both of their children have great difficulties in understanding concepts.

DISCUSSION

This case study represents a typical Haitian family in the United States. This family is trying to maintain their Haitian culture and language. Their children are also trying to use both languages for communication purposes. Also, the children were initially enrolled in bilingual programs and suddenly both of them were placed in special education classes for learning disabled children. One tends to think that perhaps these children were tested and placed in special education classes too early. Were these students demonstrating severe language disorders, or merely language differences? The observation by the parents that both children lack concept development tends to suggest that perhaps the diagnostic-prescriptive model of special education programming have relegated the children to a passive and dependent role where total control of the interaction is in the hands of the remedial instruction (Cummins, 1985). When the Instructional Team meets with the parents, the following recommendations should be discussed in order to reinforce classroom instructional activities for concept development.

1. The parents should provide opportunities for both children to explore the world through language. The children should be taken out in the neighborhood to visit places such as the zoo. While in the zoo, the parents should treat the children as partners in conversations encouraging them to take the initiative and helping them to extend the topics they initiated. Once at home, indirect exercises should be developed to

summarize the zoo visit. It is recommended that the teacher provide the parents with a list of recommended neighborhood extracurricular activities.

2. Home reinforcement activities should be presented in meaningful contexts. Dialogues about relevant topics are encouraged. During these dialogues, children should have opportunities to question the parents. Parents should provide opportunities for the encouragement of meaningful language rather than the correctness of surface forms. The teacher will send home a list of suggested topics from which the children will choose those relevant to them. These topics will include experiences to gain information and sustain social interaction.

3. Parents should be guided to see the need to listen to their children and have their children read to them. But the reading period should be meaningful to the children and to the parents. Why are the children reading to the parents? Why are the parents listening to the children's reading? A reason for the reading should be initiated at school and continued at home. Again, it is not how much reading is done, but how the reading information provides the children with an opportunity to expand cognitive skills.

Case #3

Mr. and Mrs. Chiang came from Hong Kong three years ago. Both of them work in a Chinese restaurant one hour from the home. They have three children, two of them in elementary school. The younger child is taken care of by Mr. Chiang's mother. One of the school children attends a learning disabled class. The teacher has informed Mr. and Mrs. Chiang on several occasions that their daughter, after seven months in this learning disabled class, has not been able to produce any written expression.

DISCUSSION

This Chinese family is representative of many Oriental families that have come to the United States in search of a new life. This working couple relies on the grandmother to take care of their children while they are working.

The most acute learning problem of the child participating in the special education class is a common one among students in learning disabled classes: the inability to produce written expression. The Instructional Team would recommend the following suggestions to the parents in order to reinforce the school's instructional program.

1. It is highly recommended that the teacher and the parents discuss instructional strategies for the conscious integration of language use and its development as part of all curriculum content rather than teaching language and the content as isolated subjects. It is apparent that this student has a need to develop higher level cognitive skills rather than factual recall; thus, it is possible that the student has not been motivated enough to produce creative activities. The remediation that has been provided has not permitted her to become actively involved in learning.

2. The teacher should send home exercises that provoke exploratory learning. Emphasis should not be on drill exercises which decompose learning tasks.

3. The parents should receive lists of suggested writing exercises in which the emphasis is in the presentation

of ideas rather than in the correctness of grammar and spelling. Corrections of students' writing errors and explicit teaching of grammar are not particularly effective. Smith (1983) points out that children do not learn from being corrected but from wanting to do things the right way.

CONCLUSION

There is a need to involve parents in the instructional program of limited English proficient special education students. In order to initiate and maintain parental support, it is important that parents feel a bond with the school and a significant feeling of being helpful in the instructional component of their children. School staff members enhance these feelings of being a resource person by including them in planned home activities whose main purpose is to reinforce what the school has introduced in the instructional component.

Parents, and especially those of language minority children, need guidance and specific instructional ideas to be able to perform the role of reinforcers. Teachers have to meet with them or send planned activities that the parents can follow with their children. These language activities should encourage meaningful language interaction rather than emphasize remedial instruction.

REFERENCES

Anderson, J. G., and D. Safar (1967). The influence of differential community perceptions on the provision of equal educational opportunities. *Sociology of Education,* 40, 219-230.

Baca, L. M., and H. T. Cervantes (1984). *The Bilingual Special Education Interface.* St. Louis, MO: Times Mirror/Mosby.

Cummins, J. (1985). *Bilingualism and Special Education: Issues in Assessment and Pedagogy.* San Diego, CA: College-Hill Press.

Dolson, D. (1984). The influence of various home bilingual environments on the academic achievement, language development, and psychological adjustment of fifth and sixth grade Hispanic students. Unpublished doctoral dissertation. The University of San Francisco.

Donaldson, M. (1978). *Children's Minds.* Glasgow: Collins.

Federal Register (Part II), No. 150, p. 33845, Washington, D.C., Department of Health, Education and Welfare, August, 1982.

Gearheart, B. (1985). *Learning Disabilities.* St. Louis, MO: Times Mirror/Mosby.

Hallahan, D., and W. Cruickshank (1973). *Psychoeducational Foundations of Learning Disabilities.* Englewood Cliffs, NJ: Prentice-Hall.

Krashen, S. D. (1981). *Principles and Practice in Second Language Acquisition.* Oxford: Pergamon Press.

MacNamara, J. (1966). Cognitive basis of language learning in infants. *Psychological Review,* 79, 1-13.

Myklebust, H. (1965). *Development and Disorders of Written Language.* New York: Greene and Shatton.

Oller, J. W. (1983). Testing proficiencies and diagnosing language disorders in bilingual children. In D. Omark and J. Good (Eds.), *The Bilingual Exceptional Child.* San Diego, CA: College-Hill Press.

Ortiz, A. (1985). Language and curriculum development of exceptional bilingual children. In P. Chinn (Ed.), *Education of Culturally and Linguistically Different Exceptional Children.* Reston, VA: ERI Clearinghouse on Handicapped and Gifted Children.

* * *

Schools are the battleground for the issue of whether the nation can once again embrace a new group of immigrants whose native language is not English.

ERNEST L. BOYER, president
Carnegie Foundation for the
Advancement of Teaching

5

ASSESSMENT:

Considerations Upon Interpreting Data of Linguistically/Culturally Different Students Referred for Disabilities or Disorders

Elba Maldonado-Colon

In interpreting assessment data for the culturally and linguistically different child, psychologists and diagnosticians do not seem to understand the characteristics of the second language acquisition process and their overlap with characteristics of language disorders or deficiencies among native speakers of English (Mercer, 1973; Shephard and Smith, 1981; Wright and Santa Cruz, 1983). Documented questionable special education placements involving language-minority students (Garcia, 1985; Maldonado-Colon, 1984) indicate that assessment personnel are treating language-minority children as pathological cases regardless of a language background which reflects exposure to different linguistic conditions.

In Canada, Cummins (1980) found a similar pattern among professionals involved in the evaluation of immigrant children. Cummins' data suggests that if a non-native child speaks English, regardless of its quality, he/she is automatically considered to possess the same skills and linguistic background as a native speaker of the language. That is, the child is considered proficient enough to compete with native speakers in academic areas, and is expected to perform as one. Consequently, data interpretation and program assignment are based upon a misconception which has the potential, eventually, to limit academic learnings as measured by standardized achievement tests, or worse, to lead to learning difficulties and referral to special education (Cummins, 1982).

Due to the critical impact that language proficiency has on the outcomes of psychological and educational assessments, it is imperative that professionals who diagnose problems, disorders or disabilities in linguistically/culturally different children collect as much information as possible. This information should include but not be limited to: (a) results of a language proficiency measure in each language, along with results of other measures or procedures considered appropriate to evaluate a suspected handicap or disability; (b) documentation of the language of the home as well as an estimate of the quality of language use in the home; (c) documentation of pre-academic experiences relevant to what is being evaluated; (d) records of any previous intervention in which the child was involved; and (e) the child's linguistic preference by setting (e.g., home, classroom, play area). The consideration of complete language data guides appropriate assessment, facilitates interpretation, and is essential for making the distinction between deficiencies caused by functioning in a second language, and true disorders which would be evident in the native language.

The literature suggests that the lack of descriptive and normative data for populations other than native English speakers, along with inappropriate evaluation tools, lack of trained bilingual specialists, and lack of clear policy guidelines, are factors which affect services, assessment, diagnosis and intervention for the linguistically/culturally different student (Garcia, 1986; Maldonado-Colon, 1984; Ortiz, 1984).

Taking the previous caveats into consideration, this paper attempts to: (a) question the selective use of linguistic data obtained through a biased process; (b) underscore that placement and intervention decisions are too frequently made with no consideration given to the child's exposure to a language other than English in a dual language environment, or to the consequence of mislabeling a student; and (c) emphasize the need for data related to the bilingual and limited English proficient (LEP) handicapped and nonhandicapped child.

Two studies (Garcia, 1985; Maldonado-Colon, 1984) conducted in a large metropolitan school district in the Southwest, revealed that Hispanic children identified as disordered, exhibited characteristics of second language learners. These characteristics were very similar, in most cases, to those evident among disordered native speakers of English. The linguistic similarities between the second language learners and disordered native language speakers suggested further objective and appropriate testing. However, findings of both studies indicate that additional data were not requested or considered important during the decision-making process. Results of the Maldonado-Colon (1984) study to be discussed illustrate many of the language assessment problems referred to above.

Maldonado-Colon conducted an exploratory descriptive study of randomly selected students' (special education) program folders in a district whose school population was approximately 75 percent Hispanic. Results revealed that:

1. Deviant English speech, language production, and poor academic performance were the most significant variables influencing special education referral.

71

2. Any indication that the child might be dominant in either of the languages was considered sufficient documentation to meet compliance with the determination of language dominance as required by federal legislation (Bilingual Education Act, 1972; Lau Remedies, 1974, 1975). Evidence frequently consisted of simple statements such as "The teacher says the child is Spanish dominant"; "The parent says the child speaks English at home."

3. Performance on standard English measures, developed for native speakers, served as measures of proficiency for second language learners.

4. Of the 73 Hispanics in the sample, approximately 56.2 percent (n = 41) were from homes where Spanish was spoken, while 43.8 percent (n = 32) came from homes in which English was recognized as the only language. Yet, most students were tested in English, regardless of home language or first language background.

5. Spanish measures were infrequently administered.

6. No modifications to the testing procedure, in response to different conditions affecting the population under evaluation, were reported.

7. An examination of dates when language proficiency tests were administered revealed that information as old as two years was frequently used in place of recent data.

8. Interpretation of findings disregarded the status of children as linguistically different from native speakers, thus labeling them language delayed. English language test scores among the Hispanic population reflected supposed language delays which ranged from 1.0 years

to 4.3 years, qualifying the students to receive special education services.

9. Even though some clinicians did recognize that evaluation results indicated second language learning characteristics (e.g., accent, substitutions of English sounds by Spanish sounds) and dialectal variations (e.g., phoneme substitution), they recommended placement based on the misconception that sound distortions or substitutions prevent successful reading and effective communication.

10. Upon examination of placement decisions, it was confirmed that test performance in English, along with teacher referral, were the most significant variables determining special education placement.

DISCUSSION

From the above data, it was apparent that the linguistic characteristics of bilingual and LEP Hispanics were evaluated with the same instruments utilized with native speakers of English. Further, their errors were interpreted as stringently as errors of native speakers of the language, and their placements were the same as those of native English speakers. Thus, the combination of linguistic restrictions of second language learners and phonological errors qualified these children as disordered according to the district's guidelines which were developed for use with native speakers of English. Issues such as test bias, error type, error interpretation and additional critical information required, were not addressed during the decision-making process. Disregarded was the mandate that language dominance should determine the language of assessment and the interpretation of data. Of consequence was the resulting inappropriate labeling of students as disordered when they may simply have been in the transitional phases of second language acquisition.

If the information on home language background had been taken into consideration, a significant number of children would have been tested in both languages, beginning with their dominant language. Although some children (n = 31, 42 percent) were administered Spanish language measures in addition to English measures, reflecting a degree of concern with compliance, there were no interpretations made of these scores. Information on the native language was consistently disregarded. This was evident in all program stages (e.g., referral, placement, intervention, evaluation of progress, and dismissal). Noticeable as well was the absence of a standardized procedure for testing through the native language.

CONCLUSION

Interpretations and conclusions were based on: (1) limited information with no evaluation of home language models, pre-academic experiences, and previous language instruction; (2) the premise that all English speakers constitute a homogeneous group — no recognition of the characteristics of second language learners; (3) the misconceptions that second language learners perform just like native speakers — deviant performance in the second language is equated with disordered performance; (4) inappropriate test selection — tests for native speakers were selected, with no allowances made for second language speakers, or dialectal variations; and (5) misconceptions of how language dominance is determined, or its role in the assessment process.

Recommendations for the Field

The following suggestions arise from data generated by this study. The suggestions are also supported by an increasing body of literature related to bilinguals, children of limited English proficiency, and children of limited linguistic environments:

1. Institutions of higher education should prepare all students who are to work with children to be more effective with linguistically and culturally different students.

2. Local education agencies should implement personnel development plans which include training related to the unique characteristics of the non-traditional student and how these characteristics affect test performance and data interpretation.

3. Diagnosticians required to work with populations reflecting characteristics different from those of the average student should pursue additional training intended to facilitate an optimal assessment of the specific population, to diagnose appropriately and to develop effective intervention according to diagnosed conditions.

4. Concentrated efforts should focus on the identification of best practices for referral, assessment, placement and intervention of bilingual and LEP students.

5. Whenever linguistically/culturally different children are to be assessed for the purpose of distinguishing disorders or disabilities from problems of second language acquisition, information related to the following areas should be obtained: (a) home language, including usage and characteristics; (b) time and quality of expo-

sure to English; (c) type and quality of pre-academic experience related to language and to the development of linguistic skills; and (d) type of previous instructional interventions and their outcomes. If possible, personnel should also consider the linguistic characteristics of the child's immediate community, in order to determine if those characteristics are reflected in the child's linguistic productions or language-related behaviors.

6. Information associated with language should be very carefully evaluated and should include date of elicitation and conditions of evaluation, since factors such as language development and language loss due to non-use could affect interpretation of the data.

REFERENCES

Algozzine, B.; Christenson, S.; and Ysseldyke, E. (1982). Probabilities associated with the referral to placement process. *Journal of Teacher Education, 5,* 19-23.

Burt, M. K., and Dulay, H. (1978). Some guidelines for the assessment of oral language proficiency and dominance. *TESOL QUARTERLY, 12*(2), 177-192.

Carpenter, L. (1983). *Communication Disorders in Limited- and Non-English Proficient Children.* Los Alamitos, CA: National Center for Bilingual Research.

Cummins, J. (1980). The cross-lingual dimensions of language proficiency: Implications for bilingual education and the optimal age issue. *TESOL, 14,* 175-188.

Cummins, J. (1982). Tests, achievement and bilingual students. *FOCUS, 9,* 1-6.

Dulay, H.; Burt, M.; and McKeon, D. (Eds.) (1980). *Testing and Teaching Communicatively Handicapped Hispanic Children: The State of the Art in 1980.* San Francisco, CA: Bloomsbury West.

Garcia, M. (1980). Linguistic proficiency: How bilingual discourse can show that a child has it. In R. V. Padilla (Ed.), *Ethnoperspectives in Bilingual Education Research: Theory in Bilingual Education* (62-73). Ypsilanti, MI: Eastern Michigan University.

Garcia, S. B. (1985). *Effects of Students' Characteristics, School-Program and Organi-*

zation on Decision-making for the Placement of Hispanic Students in Classes for the Learning Disabled. Doctoral dissertation, The University of Texas at Austin. UMI.

Glass, L. (1979). Coping with the bilingual child. *ASHA, 21,* 512-520.

Gonzalez, G. (1974). Language, culture and exceptional children. *Exceptional Children, 40,* 565-570.

Greenlee, M. (1981). Specifying the needs of a bilingual developmentally disabled population: Issues and case studies. *NABE Journal, 6,* 55-76.

Hamayan, E. V. (1984). *Assessment of Language Proficiency of Exceptional Bilingual Students: An Integrative Approach.* Los Alamitos, CA: National Center for Bilingual Research.

Jones, R. (1976). *Mainstreaming and the Minority Child.* Reston, VA: The Council for Exceptional Children.

Maldonado-Colon, E. (1984). *Profiles of Hispanic Students Placed in Speech, Hearing and Language Programs in a Selected School District in Texas.* Doctoral dissertation. MI: University Microfilms International (No. 84-10309).

Mercer, J. R. (1973). *Labeling the Mentally Retarded: Clinical and Social System Perspective on Mental Retardation.* Berkley, CA: University of California Press.

Ortiz, A. A. (1980). Choosing the language of instruction for exceptional bilingual children. *Teaching Exceptional Children, 16,* 208-212.

Ortiz, A. A., and Yates, J. R. (1983). Incidence of exceptionality among Hispanics: Implication for manpower planning. *NABE JOURNAL, 7,* 41-53.

Shepard, L., and Smith, M. L. (1981). *Evaluation of the Identification of Perceptual-Communicative Disorders in Colorado, Final Report.* Boulder, CO: University of Colorado.

Walters, J. (1979). Language variation in the assessment of communicative competence. In R. Silverstein (Ed.), *Occasional Papers on Linguistics No. 6* (293-303). Carbondale, IL: Southern Illinois University.

Wolfram, W. (1979). *Speech Pathology and Dialect Differences.* Arlington, VA: Center for Applied Linguistics.

Wright, P., and Santa Cruz, R. (1983). Ethnic composition of special education programs in California. *Learning Disabilities Quarterly, 6* (4), 387-394.

Language acquisition can only seem a loss for the ghetto child. . . . The child's difficulty will turn out to be psychological more than linguistic because what he gives up are symbols of home.

RICHARD RODRIGUEZ
Hunger of Memory

6

REMEDIATING READING PROBLEMS IN A HISPANIC LEARNING DISABLED CHILD FROM A PSYCHOLINGUISTIC PERSPECTIVE:

A Case Study

Diana Rivera Viera

From a psycholinguistic perspective, reading is viewed as an interaction between language and thought. In this interaction, the reader brings his/her acquired skills in language use to the reading situation. He uses these skills to make predictions about printed material. In this process the reader uses three basic kinds of information: grapho/phonic, syntactic and semantic cues. The reader makes choices which he or she thinks fit the semantic, syntactic and grapho/phonic constraints of the language in an effort to comprehend. Comprehension is the ultimate goal of reading. Therefore, reading proficiency must be defined in terms of the reader's efficiency in using the cue systems available to construct meaning.

Findings in miscue research, which examine reading from a psycholinguistic perspective, suggest that the use of reading strategies vary in poor and proficient readers. Poor readers depend most on grapho/phonic and syntactic cues in the text. Proficient readers use syntactic and semantic cues more extensively and with greater success (Goodman and Burke, 1970). Yetta Goodman (1967) suggested that the types of miscues change qualitatively as reading ability develops and comprehension tends to increase as the percentage of syntactically and semantically acceptable miscues increase.

Goodman and Burke's study (1969) found that miscues don't always result in changes in meaning. They re-emphasized the importance of analyzing miscues in terms of how they affect a reader's comprehension of the material. By analyzing a reader's oral reading miscues, it is possible to determine what reading strategies he/she is using to understand a text and their effectiveness.

Many studies in miscue research have focused on the differences in the use of cue systems by typical nonproficient and proficient readers. Several studies have examined the use of these cue systems in nonproficient and learning disabled readers. Gutknecht's study (1971) of identified perceptually handicapped children made a significant contribution by questioning the myth that perceptually handicapped children process reading in a different way than so-called "normal" children. The data indicated that the same patterns were evident in the perceptually handicapped child's oral reading behavior. Rivera-Viera (1983) found no significant differences between oral reading patterns of typical nonproficient and learning disabled Hispanic readers.

In 1972, Yetta Goodman and Carolyn Burke developed the *Reading Miscue Inventory* (RMI) as a diagnostic and evaluation instrument for reading. The instrument provides quantitative as well as qualitative information of a reader's oral reading miscues. By analyzing oral miscues made when reading a story, the teacher obtains a reader's profile of strengths and weaknesses in the use of reading strategies. The profile is an aid in developing a reading program for a particular child. It assists the teacher in selecting materials and activities which will improve reading comprehension and the effective use of the cue systems available while reading. The instrument can also be used as a pre- and post-test to evaluate the student's progress.

Based on the review of the literature in miscue research, a study was designed to use the RMI as the basis for developing a remedial reading program for a Hispanic learning disabled child. The purpose of the study was to determine if the RMI was a useful instrument in working with learning disabled (LD) readers.

THE SUBJECT

The subject (S) was a seven-year-old Puerto Rican male from a middle-class family. He was referred to the learning disabilities specialist for an educational evaluation by a psychologist. The S's first grade teacher had recommended he be retained in the first grade due to reading problems.

A summary of results provided by the psychologist's evaluation indicated that the S was impulsive, highly disorganized and very distractible. He showed an attentional deficit and had serious reversal problems when reading. His visual and graphomotor skills were those of a five-year-old. His major strengths were above-average intellectual ability, verbal and quantitative reasoning and linguistic development in general which was the level expected for an eight-year-old.

The reading material used for testing with the RMI was selected from the first grade reader *Aprendemos a leer* from the Laidlaw Reading Series *Por el mundo del cuento y la aventura* developed for Puerto Rico and other Hispanic countries in 1971. This series is used extensively by the public education system in Puerto Rico. The results of the reading profile indicated that he was ineffective in the use of reading strategies and had a 15.20 comprehension score of a possible 100 points. In terms of the use of the basic cue systems, there was a great dependence on grapho/phonic cues to the exclusion of syntactic and semantic cues. Self-correction attempts were almost nonexistent. Punctuation marks were generally ignored. His reading was merely "word calling" with no concern for trying to make sense of what was being read. His reading was so cumbersome and difficult that by the end of the story he began introducing characters and events from a previous reading primer which he had memorized. Reading was a painful experience.

THE REMEDIAL READING PROGRAM

The program consists of one hour sessions twice a week for the duration of the school year. The S worked with the learning disabilities teacher (LDT) in a separate room in the school during his language arts class. Periodic meetings were scheduled with his classroom teacher and parents to share materials and strategies used. His parents observed some of the sessions and others were recorded on tape so that they could model the intervention strategies used when working with him at home.

Oral reading exercises.

The initial RMI profile suggested that the S was "calling out words" as best he could with no regard for the fact that there was a message printed which he should try to comprehend. He became very anxious when asked to read. However, he had above-average language skills and was very articulate. He loved storytelling and his parents, who were both avid readers, had instilled in him a love for books. He had an extensive collection of children's books at home. Bedtime stories were a regular part of his nightly routine. Due to these factors, initial sessions began with oral exercises in which two of Kenneth Goodman's rules of thumb were implemented. Goodman has stated that nonproficient readers must be taught to ask themselves two questions while reading: Does this make sense? and Does it sound like language? During the first sessions, oral games were played. The LDT said to the S:

> "While we talk I will say some things which don't make sense. When I say something which doesn't sound right you will say, 'I caught you'."

Whenever the S "caught" the LDT in a mistake, he was asked to explain why it was wrong. These initial sessions involved very obvious syntactic errors such as incorrect gender correspondence or mistakes in the use of verb tense. Later, semantic errors were added. The game was then applied to mistakes made by the LDT when reading orally to the S. Once the S became aware of the importance of identifying mistakes which didn't sound right or make sense, other activities were introduced.

The S's attention span when reading was approximately five minutes at the beginning of the remedial program. This required a great deal of variation in activities within each one hour session. He would bring in toys and talk about them while he played. He also talked about activities which occurred in school and at home. While he talked, the LDT would write short paragraphs in simple language structures. The S would then be asked to read them applying the rules of thumb learned previously. He should reread anything that didn't sound right or make sense with no intervention from the LDT. Initially there was a tendency to look at the LDT whenever he was faced with a difficult word. He was encouraged to try to figure words out by saying, "You mentioned that word when you talked a while ago. Try to think of what you said. You can do it."

The use of this modified and simplified version of the language experience approach was used extensively over the school year. The classroom teacher was encouraged to use this approach instead of the reading series when working with the S. Reading time was increased to fifteen minute period with five minute recess sessions by the end of the second month.

Word reversals were frequent. Particularly with the words:

se for *es*

le for *el*

sol for *los*

al for *la*

These words are used frequently in Spanish.

When faced with these reversals, the LDT would say: "Sometimes our eyes play tricks on us. Use the questions in your mind and decide if that word fits in that sentence."

Reading storybooks from home.

The S was asked to bring in four or five of his favorite books from home. The LDT rewrote the text, simplifying the language structure. This was very important not only because of his difficulties in reading, but also because most books written in Spanish are published in Mexico, Spain or Argentina and include many regional variations of the Spanish language. In order to facilitate his application of the questions which would serve as guides, it was necessary to make the text sound like the Spanish which is used in Puerto Rico. The simplified language structures were then pasted over the original text. These stories were then used as the basic materials for a number of sessions.

When first used, the S tended to "read" the text as he had memorized it from hearing his parents read to him. When this occurred, the LDT would say:

> "What's written in print now has the same message but some of the words have been changed. You know what is going to happen because you are familiar with the story. Use that information to try to make out the words."

This strategy was very successful in improving the S's self-esteem, since he was now taking books home to read to his parents. Several variations of this strategy were introduced. First, some paragraphs were left in the original text. Then, whole pages were left in the original, and the S and LDT would take turns reading various paragraphs and pages. Reading periods were increased to twenty minutes with five minute periods for recess by the end of the fourth month.

Cloze exercises.

Cloze exercises were designed using the stories which had been modified previously. Some of the initial exercises involved deletion of specific function words (i.e., verbs, adjectives). Others involved the deletion of every nth word (i.e., 9th, 5th). Initially, the S would only accept as correct the exact word in the text. Through guided discussions he began to understand the differences in words that altered the meaning of the text and those that did not. Cloze procedure exercises interested him a great deal and increased his awareness of his skills as a language user.

Special activities for specific difficulties.

As sessions progressed, some special word attack skills were introduced to reduce the reversals and to aid in the production of sound variations which were particularly difficult. However, it should be emphasized that these activities were introduced after five months of reading in context and that at no time did they occupy more than 20 percent of the hour session. Words were rarely presented in isolation.

Reading material was designed for specific word reversals. These words were used sparingly within a text. Visual cues such as arrows were drawn over these words. Later, arrows were eliminated and substituted by verbal cues such as "Remember, don't drive against traffic." Graphs were kept to chart his progress whenever this activity was used.

There were certain sound variations which confused him. These were singled out for specific exercises. One example of this is the sound of the letter c in Spanish. When followed by *a* as in *casa* (house), *o* as in *cordon* (rope), or *u* as in *cuello* (neck), it is pronounced like *k*. When followed by *e* as in *cesped* (grass), or *i* as in *cielo* (sky), it is pronounced like *s*. Once the rule was explained and learned, reading exercises containing these sound variations were developed to provide practice.

Use of the reading series.

By the eighth month of work, textbooks were introduced. The first book used was a second grade science book. It was selected because reading material was short and had questions for discussion at the end. This allowed for reading as well as some conversation after reading. It also allowed for showing the S that he was capable of reading "advanced" materials even though he was repeating first grade.

During the ninth and last month of work, the reading series was reintroduced. He was retested with material from the second grade reader *Del campo al pueblo* from the Laidlaw Reading Series, *Por el mundo del cuento y la aventura.*

When retested with the RMI, results indicated that the S was using reading strategies which were moderately effective and his comprehension score was that of a proficient reader. The percentage of miscues which were syntactically and semantically acceptable increased, as did reading comprehension. Self-correction was present in a higher percentage than in the pre-test. In general it was demonstrated that the remedial reading program was successful, and the S was now reading with greater proficiency in terms of reading comprehension as well as in the effective use of reading strategies.

Table 1 shows the reader's profile before and after treatment. Figure 1 summarizes the percentage of miscues in terms of the degree of loss of comprehension they produced before and after treatment.

TABLE 1
RMI Profile Before and After Treatment

Reader Profile	Pre-test	Post-test
Comprehension Score	15.20	82.70
Syntactically Acceptable Miscues	4%	42%
Semantically Acceptable Miscues	3%	41%
Self-correction Attempts	1%	47%

SUMMARY AND CONCLUSIONS

The RMI was found to be a useful instrument in developing a remedial reading program for a Hispanic learning disabled child. By examining the use of reading strategies used by the LD reader, it was possible to select reading activities and materials to improve his reading comprehension. The study suggests that a reader's profile and not a learning disabilities categorization is a more useful guide in the selection of reme-dial reading activities.

The examination of reading behavior from a psycholinguistic perspective is an alternative for professionals working with the learning disabled. More studies applying a psycholinguistic model of reading to learning disabled readers would allow broadening the generalization of its usefulness in working with this population.

BEFORE TREATMENT

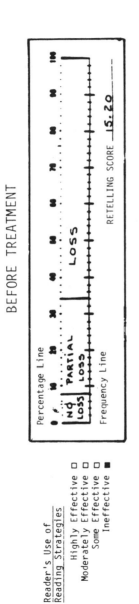

Reader's Use of
Reading Strategies

Highly Effective ☐
Moderately Effective ☐
Some Effective ☐
Ineffective ■

AFTER TREATMENT

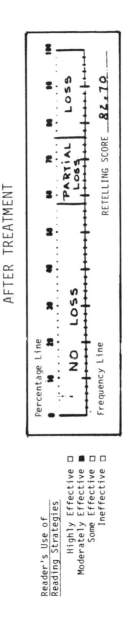

Reader's Use of
Reading Strategies

Highly Effective ☐
Moderately Effective ■
Some Effective ☐
Ineffective ☐

FIGURE 1

Percentage of Miscues Made During Oral Reading which Caused no Loss, Partial or Total Loss of Comprehension

REFERENCES

Goodman, K. S., and Burke, C. L. A study of oral reading miscues that result in grammatical re-transformations. (U.S.O.E. Final Report, Project No. 7-E-219) Contract No. OEG-0-8-070219-2806(010). Washington, D.C.: U.S. Department of Health, Education and Welfare, June 1969.

Goodman, K. S., and Burke, C. L. When a child reads: A psycholinguistic analysis. *Elementary English,* 1970, *47,* 121–129.

Goodman, Y. M. A psycholinguistic description of observed oral reading phenomena in selected young beginning readers. Unpublished doctoral dissertation, Wayne State University, 1967.

Goodman, Y. M., and Burke, C. L. *Reading Miscue Inventory: Procedure for Diagnosis and Evaluation.* New York: Macmillan, 1972.

Gutnecht, B. A psycholinguistic analysis of the oral reading behavior of selected children identified as perceptually handicapped. Unpublished doctoral dissertations, Wayne State University, 1971.

Por el mundo del cuento y la aventura. Palo Alto, CA: Laidlaw Brothers, 1971.

Rivera-Viera, D. Lectura oral de ninos con problemas de aprendizaje. *Apuntes,* 1983, *4*(2), 24.

The fact is that there is no proven method of bilingual education that guarantees fluency.

ALBERT SHANKER, president
American Federation of Teachers

7

A MULTIDISCIPLINARY MODEL TO EDUCATE MINORITY LANGUAGE STUDENTS WITH HANDICAPPING CONDITIONS

Carmen Simich-Dudgeon

INTRODUCTION

In the past decade, a growing number of minority language students, both limited-English proficient (LEP) and non-English proficient (NEP) have enrolled in our public schools. Instructional programs such as bilingual education and English-as-a-second-language (ESL) have been developed to teach them language and cultural concepts they need to fully benefit from educational opportunities available to them through our public education system.

Two landmark decisions contributed to progress made regarding the education of LEP/NEP students. The Bilingual Education Act of 1968 provided a legal recourse to address the needs of language minority children through bilingual instruction. In 1975, the U.S. Office of Education and the Office of Civil Rights jointly issued what became known as the "Lau Remedies" (HEW Memorandum, 1975). This document outlined procedures for the identification and placement of LEP/NEP students in programs appropriate to their linguistic and educational needs. Bilingual instruction was mandated as the only acceptable intervention on behalf of LEP/NEP students (Bergin, 1980).

At the present time, the definition of an appropriate educational intervention has been expanded to include alternative programs, such as ESL under Public Law 98-511 (Bilingual Education Act Amendments, 1985).

The rights of handicapped children to equal educational opportunities have also been the focus of attention in the last decade and have culminated with the enactment of Public Law 94-142 (1975) as part B of the Education of the Handicapped Act. This and another landmark decision, the Vocational Rehabilitation Act, Section 504 (1973) required that all handicapped children be provided a free and appropriate public education. Begin (1980) states that LEP/NEP students:

> are not necessarily exceptional or handicapped children. Although they may be entitled to bilingual and English-as-a-second-language programs in order to learn to their full capacity, such programs are not considered special education programs. However, these children may also be handicapped or exceptional and thus entitled to have bilingual/ESL assistance and special education services. (p. 9)

The education of handicapped LEP/NEP students is just beginning to be seriously considered as school districts develop programs that attempt to meet these students' needs. Lack of research and dissemination of promising practices have contributed to confusion and a lack of understanding of what should constitute an appropriate educational intervention for these students. A recent study of mainstreamed LEP handicapped students in bilingual programs (Vasques Nuttall Associates, 1983) found that services varied from one local education agency (LEA) to another and that wherever bilingual special education is not available LEP handicapped students tend to remain in bilingual class-rooms without a formal Individualized Education Plan (IEP) and without being formally identified as handicapped. (p. ii)

The Vasquez Nuttall study also found that "for non-Hispanic LEP handicapped students, bilingual special education pro-grams are rare" (p. ii). Over-representation of LEP/NEP stu-dents in special education classes, particularly in classes for the mentally retarded, has been documented (Mercer, 1973). Furthermore, there is controversy about identification and assess-ment procedures used to place LEP/NEP students in special education programs, with most of the criticism being directed at issues of cultural bias in psychological tests and validity and reliability of currently used English proficiency tests (Bergin, 1980; Hisama, 1980; Simich and Rivera, 1981, 1983).

Other concerns are the need to train teachers in both ESL/bilingual education and special education and to promote the interface of both disciplines in the education of LEP handi-capped students (Bergin, 1980). The Vasques Nuttall study found that "the focus of most inservice training for special education personnel was on legal requirements, identification and referral procedures" (p. ii). This finding suggests that school districts do not generally consider curriculum cultural and/or linguistic inservice training as priority issues. Concerns regarding legal and procedural matters have overshadowed these important educational issues. In addition, adequacy of curriculum and materials development for the LEP handicapped have so far received minimal attention at the local school level.

Research on LEP/NEP children is scarce. The Handicapped Minority Research Institute located in Los Alamitos, California, is one of the few institutions whose main goal is to conduct applied research on the education of the mildly handicapped LEP/NEP student and research training for graduate students (Bender, 1984). During 1984, the following research efforts were being implemented:

> *Longitudinal Study 1:* explores districts' policies and strategies in the education of Hispanic LEP with special needs. The Institute will develop a best practices model to assist other districts in providing a quality education to language minority students.
>
> *Longitudinal Study 2:* focuses on high school students' communicative needs at school and in future work settings.
>
> *Short-term Studies:* focus on assessment practices, strategies for communicating with parents of LEP handicapped and the participation of these students in mainstreamed educational programs.

EDUCATION MODELS FOR
LEP HANDICAPPED STUDENTS

Ambert and Dew (1982) proposed three educational models for the education of LEP students with special needs:

1. *The Bilingual Support Model:* an English-speaking special education teacher, trained in ESL methods, implements the student's IEP with the assistance of a bilingual aide. The aide reinforces educational concepts in the student's native language.

2. *The Coordinated Services Model:* students are serviced

by accredited special education and bilingual/ESL teachers who have been trained in the foundations and methods of both disciplines. Both teachers work as a team. The special education teacher is responsible for services delivered in English and the bilingual teacher instructs bilingually or in the student's native language.

3. *The Integrated Bilingual/Special Education Model*: one accredited bilingual teacher with training in both bilingual education and special education delivers all services.

These and other educational approaches are being used in the education of LEP handicapped students (Bergin, 1980). However, a comprehensive account of educational programs is not available (Bender, 1985). Some of the issues that need to be seriously considered are:

- The need for a multidisciplinary theoretical framework to develop valid, culturally and linguistically appropriate educational interventions for LEP/NEP handicapped.

- The need to develop appropriate educational programs that serve *all* LEP/NEP handicapped students, regardless of their native language. Programs for LEP/NEP handicapped should not be confined to a bilingual model of instruction. Other educational approaches, such as ESL, should be considered for practical and educational reasons. One of these is the shortage of bilingual special education professionals to provide services to *all* LEP/NEP handicapped students. In Fairfax County Public Schools, Fairfax County, Virginia, LEP students speak over seventy different languages. When only bilingual education is implemented, only a few LEP/NEP handicapped can be appropriately serviced (Vasques Nuttall Associates, 1983). Another reason is that there continues to be controversy regarding the effectiveness of the bilingual and ESL models of instruction for minority language students.

- The need for collaboration among all professionals serving LEP/NEP handicapped students.

- The need for continued applied research and dissemination of information regarding promising practices and/or programs of excellence for LEP/NEP exceptional students.

A MULTIDISCIPLINARY MODEL FOR LEP/NEP HANDICAPPED STUDENTS

A pilot program was implemented during the 1984-85 school year in Fairfax County Public Schools (FCPS) to service the growing population of LEP/NEP students with special needs. The writer was hired as an ESL/Special Education resource teacher to develop and implement this program. The basic tenet underlying the nature and scope of the pilot was PL 94-142. The law mandates that all handicapped students, including those with limited-English proficiency, are entitled to participate in and benefit from any appropriate program or activity to which they would otherwise be entitled if they were not handicapped. Tenets from pedagogy, sociolinguistics and ethnography strongly influenced what became the Multidisciplinary Model. These tenets recognize that:

- The appropriate education of LEP/NEP handicapped necessitates the cooperation of professionals working with these students. In particular, it necessitates the collaboration between ESL and special education teachers and administrators. It is believed that a team approach maximizes the opportunities for these students to reach their potential and increases the sharing of much needed professional information. A cooperative, collaborative framework is considered indispensable in the development of an appropriate educational model for LEP exceptional students.

- Professionals trained in both ESL/special education are needed to coordinate and implement the program. Furthermore, all special education and ESL teachers must be trained in the foundations and methods of ESL and special education.

- Observation and description of the student in selected teaching situations is considered essential before programmatic changes are recommended. The ESL/Special Education resource teacher develops recommendations on the basis of observations of the student's communicative strategies during face-to-face interaction with the teacher and his/her peers; his/her literacy skills; interviews with the teacher and student and review of files. Her recommendations should be focused on language-related goals that support existing IEP goals for the student.

- The evaluation of the program should incorporate data from both qualitative and quantitative sources such as results from observations and language proficiency tests, respectively.

A Multidisciplinary Model was developed by the ESL/Special Education resource teacher.

The Model provided a continuum of ESL services, from consultative to direct instruction on the basis of the following student variables:

- Whether or not the student has received ESL instruction

- The number of years of ESL instruction

- The level of English language proficiency. FCPS, for example, considers three levels: advanced (B_2), intermediate (B_1) and beginner or non-English proficient (A).

Consultative services were defined as resource services for special education teachers with a focus on the English language goals of the student. Consultative services for students included interviews during which student input and collaboration was sought. The purpose of the interviews was to make the student aware of the need for his/her active involvement and his/her potential to learn the second language.

Direct instructional services were defined as a series of ESL instructional options for direct student instruction. These options included:

- ESL instruction in a regular ESL classroom

- Special ESL classes. These are small-group classes where the LEP handicapped student was given individualized language instruction.

- ESL instruction in other than the above, e.g., itinerant ESL instruction, volunteer services and ESL/Special Education resource teacher instruction.

Services other than the above were decided on a one-to-one

basis by an ESL administrator based on recommendations from the resource teacher and the special education teacher. The initial Multidisciplinary Model provides a detailed account of all instructional options considered (see Table 1).

Results from the 1984-85 pilot were reviewed by a committee of special educators and ESL educators, including the writer. Their recommendations were further reviewed and finalized by administrators from ESL and special education. A modified Multidisciplinary Model emerged. The revised Model maintained the legal and theoretical framework that characterized the initial model, but changes were made to clarify instructional options and procedures. The revised model had one specific objective: to improve the functional English proficiency of students who qualify for special education services who are limited or non-English proficient through a coordinated effort between Special Education and ESL.

REFERRAL AND EVALUATION PROCEDURES

Procedures were developed for distribution to both ESL and Special Education teachers and administrators.

1. Special Education teachers who suspect a LEP/NEP student has learning difficulties related to a lack of English proficiency will refer the student to the school principal.

2. The school principal will send a written referral to the ESL administrator with a copy to the Special Education administrator. Student information to be included is date of referral, student name, age, grade and identification (I.D.) number; special education placement; ESL status (i.e., B_2, B_1, A or not in ESL); brief descrip-

TABLE 1
Level of ESL/Special Education Services

Students	Years in ESL Program	Level of Language Proficiency.	ESL Services
		B-2	Consultative and/or Other Services
	Over 2 years	B-1	Consultative and Other Services
		A	Consultative and/or Direct Instruction
Students who have received		B-2	Consultative AND Direct Instruction
or are receiving	2 years	B-1	Consultative and Other Services
ESL services		A	Consultative and/or Direct Instruction
		B-2	Consultative AND Direct Instruction
	1 year or less	B-1	Consultative and Other Services
		A	Consultative and/or Direct Instruction
			Consultative AND Direct Instruction
Students who have		B-2	Consultative and Other Services
not received ESL	0 years	B-1	Consultative and/or Direct Instruction
services		A	Consultative AND Direct Instruction

tion of the language problem and name of the school and teacher making the referral.

3. When the referral is received, the ESL/Special Education resource teacher will contact the referring school and arrange with the teacher a date to observe the student, preferably in language-related activities. At least two observations will be conducted. The focus of the observations must be the student's communication and social skills during interaction with teachers and peers. The resource teacher will review all records including ESL history and testing information. Additional language proficiency testing will be recommended if appropriate.

4. A conference between the ESL/Special Education resource teacher and the referring teacher will be held within two weeks following the final observation. The resource teacher will invite all staff working with the student and will share written suggestions for language-related activities from an ESL perspective.

5. The level of ESL services will be determined by all involved personnel. The services will support the existing special education program for the student.

6. Follow-up meetings will be scheduled and the special education and resource teachers will continue working together.

7. When the student moves from one school to another, the ESL/Special Education information will be sent with other records to ensure continuity of services.

8. In addition to suggestions for changes in IEP language-related goals, the resource teacher provides ESL strategies, materials and cultural information that might

TABLE 2
Level of ESL/Special Education Services

Students	Years in ESL Program	Level of Language Proficiency.	ESL Services
Students who have received or are receiving ESL services.	Over 2 years	B-2 B-1 A	Consultative/Resource Services — *Consultative services* are provided to special education teacher(s) which focus on language goals of the student. — *Resource services* are decided by ESL coordinator based on recommendations from the ESL/Special Education resource teacher and the special education teacher. Such services might include interpreter/translation services, liaison with the home and other short term interventions.

	2 years or less	B-2	Consultative/Resource services
		B-1	Consultative/Resource services
		A	Consultative/Resource services and/or Direct Instruction

Direct Instruction

- ESL instruction in a regular ESL classroom
- Special ESL class (small group)
- Itinerant ESL teacher
- ESL/Special Education resource teacher
- Reinforcement activities provided by volunteers (when appropriate)

Students who have not received ESL services	0 years	B-2	Consultative and Other Services
		B-1	Consultative and/or Direct Instruction
		A	Consultative AND Direct Instruction

improve communication between the student, his/her family and the teacher. A description of the revised Model is shown on Table 2.

SUMMARY AND RECOMMENDATIONS

The Multidisciplinary Model is a unique approach developed on the basis of legal, pedagogical, sociolinguistic and ethnographic principles. The Model emphasizes the need for a collaborative and cooperative approach as essential for teaching students whose needs go beyond the expertise of individual professionals. The use of qualitative techniques, such as structured observations and interviews, were at the heart of the implementation process. Results from the first year of the pilot program indicate that special education teachers welcomed information about the teaching of a second language, strategies for use with LEP/NEP students, and the coordination of efforts among all professionals involved in the education of their LEP/NEP handicapped students.

The Multidisciplinary Model is the result of the concern of FCPS educators to provide equal educational opportunities for LEP/NEP handicapped students. Recommendations from the pilot will result in the training of both special education and ESL teachers to include foundations and methods from both disciplines. The Model will also be expanded to include LEP/NEP students who are enrolled in ESL classes but who are being considered for special education. In addition, FCPS documents which have been translated in other languages will be made available to special education teachers, and a file of translated special education documents will continue to be expanded.

REFERENCES

Ambert, A., and Dew, N. *Special Education for Exceptional Bilingual Students.* Dallas, TX: Evaluation, Dissemination and Assessment Center, 1982.

Bender, J. The education of all handicapped students. In *Educating the Language Minority Student: Classroom and Administrative Issues.* Rosslyn: National Clearinghouse for Bilingual Education, 1984.

Bender, J. Personal communication, June 5, 1985.

Bergin, V. *Special Education Needs in Bilingual Programs.* Rosslyn: National Clearinghouse for Bilingual Education, 1980.

Bilingual Education Act, 20, U.S.C.880 (b): Washington, D.C., Education Department, January 2, 1968.

Bilingual Education Act Educational Amendments of 1984. P.L. 98-511: Washington, D.C., Education Department, October 1984.

Education of Handicapped Children Act, P.L. 94-142: Washington, D.C., U.S. Congress, 1975.

Hisama, K. K. An analysis of various ESL/proficiency tests. In J. W. Oller, Jr., and K. Perkins (Eds.), *Research in Language Testing.* Rowley, MA: Newbury House Publishing, Inc., 1980.

Mercer, J. R. *Labelling the Mentally Retarded.* Berkeley, CA: University of California Press, 1973.

Simich, C., and Rivera, C. Teacher training and ethnographic/sociolinguistic issues in the assessment of bilingual students' language proficiency. In C. Rivera (Ed.), *An Ethnographic/Sociolinguistic Approach to Language Proficiency.* Clevendon, England: Multilingual Matters, Ltd., 1983.

Simich, D., and Rivera, C. Issues in the assessment of the language proficiency of limited-English-proficient students. *NABA Journal,* 1981, V(3).

Vasquez Nuttall Associates, Inc. *A Study of Mainstreamed LEP Handicapped Students in Bilingual Education.* Newton, Massachusetts, 1983.

ACKNOWLEDGEMENTS

The author is especially indebted to the following Fairfax County Public School administrators: Dr. Esther Eisenhower, ESL Coordinator, Dr. Sammie M. Campbell, Director, Office of

Special Education Programs, and Dr. Margaret True, Coordinator, Special Education, Area I, for their support of the program and their valuable contributions to the revised program. Rebecca Moscoso, ESL/Special Education resource teacher, worked with the author during the implementation of the program. Her professional experience and dedication contributed greatly to the success of the program. Other professionals deserve recognition for their work of revising the program, on the basis of their experience and results from the pilot: Ann Heck, Secondary Program Specialist, LD/MMR; Alicia Clelland, Secondary Specialist, LD/MMR; Dr. Margaret True, Coordinator, Special Education; Rebecca Moscoso, ESL/Special Education resource teacher; Paula Olson, ESL Diagnostician. Any oversights or errors in these pages, however, are the author's own.

I don't deny my heritage as a Mexican-American, but the reason that we have achieved what we have in this country is that we speak English.

ARTHUR M. VASQUEZ, contractor
Fillmore United School District
California

8

POLICY ISSUES ASSOCIATED WITH SERVING BILINGUAL EXCEPTIONAL CHILDREN

Shernaz B. Garcia and James R. Yates

Rather dramatic changes are occurring in the demography of this country. An examination of the changes in the U.S. resident population by race between the 1970 and 1980 U.S. census years reflects that the white or Anglo population has declined from 83 percent to 76.8 percent, while the Hispanic population has increased from 4.5 percent to 6.4 percent, with the black population remaining relatively stable at 11.1 percent to 11.7 percent. Of greater importance to educators is the fact that public school enrollment reflects parallel changes relative to its ethnic composition; i.e., between 1972 and 1983, white student enrollment declined by 4.6 percent, while enrollments rose by 42.9 percent for Hispanics and 38.7 percent for blacks (Feistritzer, 1985).

For educators the significance of this changing demography in the public school population becomes even more obvious when an examination is made of the median age of white, black and Hispanic populations. The median age represents a measure of the child bearing potential and, in turn, of projected enrollments of school age children of each ethnic group. Specifically, the median age of white citizens of this country is over 31 years, the median age of black citizens is almost 24 years, and for Hispanics just over 21 years of age. The implication is obvious: In the future, public school populations will continue to reflect greater numbers of minority students.

Some may hold the perception that this increased minority school population is an isolated or geographically centered phenomenon, such as in the Southwest or the Southeast. However, it should be pointed out that in 1982, 49.2 percent of public school students in New Jersey, 56.3 percent of students in California, 32 percent in New York, 33 percent in Maryland, 49 percent in New Mexico, and 58.5 percent of the public school students in Illinois were of minority background. In fact, in all but two of the 25 largest public school systems in this country, more than half of the students are minority.

One of the great concerns in recent years, as reflected in the literature and in public policy statements, is the decline in SAT scores for students in this country. While there has been some encouragement about small increases in average SAT scores, it is interesting to note that most of this increase can be related to increases in the scores of minorities, not of whites. However, as reflected in Figure 1, there is a direct relationship between SAT achievement and median family income, particularly for the largest ethnic minority groups in this country—black, Mexican-American and Puerto Rican (Feistritzer, 1985).

These educational effects by ethnicity become explicit when examining the percentage of students graduating. For example, in the state of Texas, 78 percent of the white population graduates from high school. However, while Texas has had the fastest growing Hispanic population (33.5 percent increase) within public schools in the past ten years, the number of Hispanic high school graduates is slightly more than one-half,

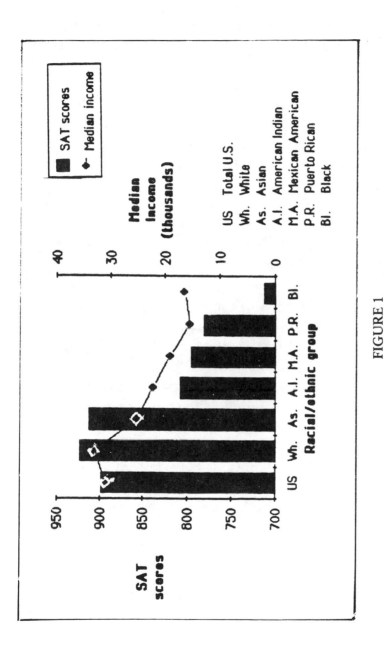

FIGURE 1

Relationship between SAT Scores and median family income by racial/ethnic group, 1984.

Note: Adapted by permission from *"Cheating Our Children: Why We Need School Reform"* (p. 10) by C. E. Feistritzer, 1985, Washington, D.C.: National Center for Education Information. Copyright 1985 by the National Center for Education Information.

with only 56.7 percent of Hispanic students completing high school. The conclusion appears clear: The fastest growing population group is also the group with which the schools of Texas are having the least success in educating. Success in educational institutions for minorities in this country steadfastly diminishes in dramatic fashion as one progresses to higher levels of the educational enterprise (see Table 1).

There is a clear relationship between education and earning power in this country. As has been seen, the educational attainment of the different ethnic groups is dramatically lower compared to whites, as is the median income by ethnic group. In 1982, the median income of the white population of this country was $21,117. The median income was $15,178 for Hispanics, and $11,968 for blacks. These data become even more critical when related to the trend associated with high school graduation. For example, in 1975 Hispanics reflected 57.5 percent graduating from high school. By 1980 that percentage had declined to 53.7 percent. In 1975 the percentage of Hispanics enrolling in college was 35.4 percent; by 1980 it had declined to 29.9 percent (McNett, 1983).

One of the adaptations made by the educational enterprise to serve students who do not make ordinary progress in the educational system is the special education system. Special education represents a unique component of the educational system as it is driven by federal and state legal mandates, and explicit policies and procedures associated with steps for entry to and exit from special education programs. It reflects a history of concern, including litigation, associated with the service delivery of special education to minority students. A study by Ortiz and Yates (1983) has pointed out the discrepant

TABLE 1
Persistence in Higher Education by Racial or Ethnic Group

	Percentage Who:				
	Complete High School	Enter College	Complete College	Enter Graduate or Professional School	Complete Graduate or Professional School
Whites	83	38	23	14	8
Blacks	72	29	12	8	4
Chicanos	55	22	7	4	2
Puerto Ricans	55	25	7	4	2
American Indians	55	17	6	4	2

Note: From *Minorities in American Higher Education* (p. 51) by A. W. Austin, 1982, San Francisco, CA: Jossey-Bass, Inc. Copyright 1982 by Jossey-Bass, Inc. Reprinted with permission.

representation of minorities within special education programs from the expected nation-wide norm. Specifically, there is dramatic over-representation of Hispanics in programs for learning disabled and the communication disordered in Texas. In order to understand this phenomenon, it is necessary to investigate and closely review the operating practices associated with serving minorities within special education.

Historically, large numbers of minority students have been placed in special education (Mercer, 1973; Tucker, 1980). Federal data indicate that 44 percent of all Hispanics in special education are in programs for the learning disabled (LD), followed by 30.2 percent in speech. In their study of incidence for Hispanics in special education in Texas, Ortiz and Yates (1983) showed that, with the exception of LD programs, Hispanics are under-served in special education. Eighty percent of Hispanic handicapped students are in LD and speech programs, with three times as many students in LD as might be expected from their representation in the school enrollment.

The research literature on placement of students in special education identifies several factors which influence decision-makers as well as the decision-making process (Blaschke, 1979; Ortiz and Yates, 1983; Stearns, Green, and David, 1980). In brief, these may include some or all of the following: policy and law; variability in state and local definitions of the handicap; litigation; availability of human, material, and financial resources in the district; shortage of assessment personnel; and inadequate procedures—including bias in the referral and assessment process. Special education services to language minority students may additionally be affected by a lack of bilingual programs and personnel, and increased awareness and understanding of issues and research related to bilingualism and other unique student attributes.

A DOCUMENTED NEED FOR
IMPROVED POLICY AND PRACTICE

Studies of Hispanic learning disabled and speech impaired students in Texas (Garcia, 1984; Maldonado-Colon, 1984) and perceptual-communicative disordered students in Colorado (Shepard and Smith, 1981) have revealed that the reasons for referral to, and placement in, these programs are often related to the acquisition of English as a second language, and/or that referring teachers may be unable to distinguish a true language disorder from the developmental process of acquiring a second language.

In her research, discussed in detail below, Garcia (1984) focused specifically on district policies and practices related to the identification and placement of 111 Hispanic and non-Hispanic students in LD programs in an urban school district in Texas. Student characteristics were compared by ethnicity, as were variables such as membership of students' referral and placement committees, assessment practices, and the nature of services recommended. Information was also sought related to the educational background, training and experience of 131 school district personnel involved in the referral, assessment and placement process for the students in the sample.

Characteristics of Hispanic LD Students

For all students in the sample (Hispanic and non-Hispanic), the most frequent reasons for referral were problems in reading and language. Referring teachers did not appear to make

119

decisions based on the Hispanic student's primary language and/or history of bilingual education, if any. This distinction may be an important one since 39 percent of all placements in compensatory education were in bilingual and/or English as a Second Language (ESL) programs for Hispanics in the sample, in addition to an equal number in Title I/Chapter 1 reading and math.

While behavior problems were not a frequent reason for the referral of Hispanic students, an interesting difference was noted in the nature of problems reported for these children. Hispanic students were more likely to experience problems in the areas of attention and order, or relations with adults and authority. More detailed analyses are needed to investigate this difference and to identify the specific behaviors under these general categories. Future research should consider the possibility that certain culturally determined behaviors manifested by Hispanic students may be interpreted as inappropriate within the school environment. Additionally, certain behavior "problems," such as inattention and inability to follow directions, may well be the result of the limited English proficient student's failure to understand the instructions or activities in the classroom.

Linguistic data were available for approximately half the Hispanic sample, and usually consisted of the *Language Assessment Scales* (LAS) (Duncan and DeAvila, 1981). Since this information was inconsistent, outdated or incomplete, comparisons of referral and assessment data by language proficiency or dominance were limited or not possible. Where this information *was* available, Hispanics appeared to demonstrate low levels of English proficiency (see Table 2).

TABLE 2
Performance of Hispanic Learning Disabled Students on the Language Assessment Scales

Scales and Levels	No. (%) of Students	
LAS–English (N = 38)		
Level 1 Non-English	17	(44.7)
Level 2 Non-English	4	(10.5)
Level 3 Bilingual	7	(18.4)
Level 4 Near Fluent, English	6	(15.8)
Level 5 Fluent English Speaker	4	(10.5)
LAS–Spanish (N = 28)		
Level 1 Non-Spanish	13	(46.4)
Level 2 Non-Spanish	8	(28.6)
Level 3 Bilingual	2	(7.1)
Level 4 Near Fluent, Spanish	3	(10.7)
Level 5 Fluent Spanish Speaker	2	(7.1)

Low English proficiency appeared to influence the test performance of Hispanic students who consistently scored lower than non-Hispanics on all subtests of the Verbal Scale of the *Wechsler Intelligence Scale for Children—Revised* (WISC-R) (Wechsler, 1974), except the arithmetic subtest, and who were thus more likely to have Full Scale IQ scores below 80. In contrast, they performed as well as non-Hispanic students on the Performance Scale and also had similar achievement test profiles. Finally, because of the depressed scores on the Verbal

Scale, Hispanic students frequently showed discrepancies of 15 points or more between the Verbal and Performance Scales of the WISC–R (see Table 3).

Based on these evaluation results, Hispanic students, like their non-Hispanic peers, were placed in LD resource programs for reading and language instruction. However, an important difference in special education services was found in the provision of related services and the identification of a secondary handicap. Only Hispanics were found to be identified as LD/SH and were receiving speech therapy as a related service. Non-Hispanic students usually received counseling or other related services. Though this study did not investigate the nature of speech problems for Hispanic students, Maldonado-Colon (1984) showed that many problems identified as speech handicaps tend to be related to articulation and second language acquisition.

COMPARISONS OF SPECIAL
EDUCATION POLICY AND PRACTICE

The district's policy manual for special education reflected an awareness and knowledge of desired professional practices and procedural safeguards related to the identification of handicapping conditions for minority students. However, greater emphasis is needed on procedures affecting limited English proficient (LEP) and/or bilingual students during the process of referral, assessment and placement. Discrepancies between district policy and professional practice were noted in several areas, suggesting that district guidelines may not provide school personnel with adequate direction, especially given the shortage of professionals with the relevant training and experience

TABLE 3
Mean Scaled Scores and IQ on the Verbal and Performance Scales of the WISC–R by Ethnicity

Scale/Subtest	Hispanic	Non-Hispanic
Verbal Scale Scores (N = 89)		
Information	5.6*	7.0
Similarities	7.0**	9.4
Arithmetic	7.7	8.2
Vocabulary	7.1**	8.9
Comprehension	7.7**	9.9
Digit Span (N = 62)	6.1**	7.9
Sum of Scaled Scores	35.3***	43.8
Performance Scale Scores (N = 92)		
Picture Completion	9.9	9.8
Picture Arrangement	9.4	10.3
Block Design	9.6	8.8
Object Assembly	10.4	10.2
Coding	9.2	8.4
Mazes (N = 13)	11.0	10.2
Sum of Scaled Scores	48.4	47.5
Verbal Scale IQ	81.6	92.1
Performance Scale IQ	97.9	96.4
Full Scale IQ		

Note: $*p < .05$ $**p < .01$ $***p < .005$

to work with language minority, handicapped students. Often, data required to be gathered were missing or reported inadequately. For Hispanic students, these missing data included language proficiency and dominance information.

Assessment practices revealed a standard approach to all students, in terms of the number and types of tests used, the language of administration, as well as interpretation of the results. For the vast majority, the identification of LD as the primary handicap was based on results from three to four tests: the WISC–R, the *Wide Range Achievement Test* (WRAT) (Jastak and Jastak, 1978) and/or the *Peabody Individual Achievement Test* (PIAT) (Dunn and Markwardt, 1970), and the *Bender Visual Motor Gestalt Test* (Koppitz, 1975). Only 12 out of 74 administrations were reported as bilingual for Hispanic students; however, no details were recorded about administration, scoring or interpretation, making this information difficult to interpret.

Finally, the analysis of practices revealed limited or no participation of other special program personnel in the referral, assessment and placement processes. Referral committees were usually composed of the principal, the counselor, and regular and special education teachers. Admission, Review, and Dismissal (ARD) committees were similarly composed of administrative, appraisal and instructional representatives from regular and special education, but rarely documented the presence of professional staff from the bilingual education, ESL or Chapter 1 programs.

Program Availability

The availability of other special programs as an option to special education did not appear to be an issue in this district, as Title I/Chapter 1 and bilingual education services were available in all schools included in this study. However, eligibility criteria for such programs were based on achievement tests that were not usually included in the special education review process. In the absence of this test information and the limited participation of personnel from these programs in the decision-making processes of special education, students are less likely to be identified as eligible for such services even when they qualify. Greater collaboration is needed between programs in order to improve service delivery for students who need bilingual special education.

Personnel

Information gathered on a sample of 131 district personnel showed that, in contrast to the high (77 percent) Hispanic enrollment in the district, the personnel sample was predominantly non-Hispanic. A little over half were assessment or supervisory personnel, including educational diagnosticians, school psychologists, counselors, speech therapists and special education supervisors. The rest were special program instructional staff. Although the data revealed a relatively high number of dual endorsements in LD and bilingual education, the proportion of Spanish-speaking individuals was low, with no information about their level of Spanish proficiency. It should be noted that Spanish-speaking skills alone cannot improve assessment or instructional quality unless accompanied by training in issues related to bilingualism and language.

Implications for Policy and Administrative Practice

Results of the Garcia (1984) study indicate that there is a general need to re-examine and revise current special education policies and guidelines to improve the processes of identification and decision-making related to limited English proficient handicapped students. The following recommendations are made to assist school districts in developing policies and guidelines to improve services for language minority handicapped students.

Identification and Placement

1. Districts need explicit policy in the arena of "child find" as the possibility exists for handicapped Hispanic students to remain unidentified based upon the culturally-based reluctance of the family to allow someone other than the family to assume responsibility and/or the obligation for the care of a handicapped child. Even the concept of placing the child within the responsibility of the school could be a problem which would necessitate policy that would assure the participation of appropriate school personnel with cultural understanding and language proficiency in the community to help identify handicapped students who might not otherwise come to the attention of the school.

2. Based upon the documentation of current practices, it seems particularly important for school districts to develop policy which makes it clear that referral to special education is the "last step" and is utilized only after all other interventions have been attempted. These might include assessment of language proficiency and the identification of the effects of language proficiency and dominance, utilization of bilingual and/or ESL instruction, and re-teaching of the basic concepts. Conceptually, the special education model is the "continuum of services" model, which indicates that spe-

126

cial education is, in fact, more restrictive in terms of the concept of normalization than other interventions.

3. As referral to special education occurs, districts must have policies which assure that assessment is accomplished by trained qualified assessors utilizing assessment materials and procedures which match the child's current language dominance. The comprehensive assessment should not be initiated or accomplished prior to an effective language assessment, and the assessment process must match the language dominance determined through that assessment.

4. School districts need to have policy in place and procedures implemented to assure that the various placement or decision-making committees have the skill to interpret assessment data in light of the language and culture of the child when dealing with LEP or bilingual children. Specifically, this implies the presence and participation of an individual on the placement committee who is more than a mere interpreter to the parent, who knows the various options within the educational system, and who understands the orientation of bilingual education, ESL, regular education and special education. For most districts, it may be more efficacious to develop the knowledge and understanding of special education programs among bilingual education personnel, than to have special educators attempt to learn and understand the implications of a second language and culture.

Programs

There are specific program implications for school districts:

1. District policy needs to be quite explicit that it is the right of the bilingual or limited English proficient handi-

capped student to have the same access to the range of special education services as any other handicapped student. For example, a student in bilingual education who is ascertained to be handicapped should have access to special education services.

2. Districts need to have policies which indicate that it is not only appropriate but essential to provide special education instructional methodologies to the limited English proficient bilingual student who is handicapped. If special education has special procedures that are efficacious for improving the learning of handicapped students, there is clear logic and obligation to provide such special methodologies of instruction and materials to the handicapped youngster who is also of limited English proficiency or bilingual.

3. There should be clear district policy that there can and should be linkages and interface between regular education (including various compensatory education programs, such as Chapter 1), bilingual education and special education. These programs should not be seen as isolated or free standing programs when it comes to serving the limited English proficient or bilingual handicapped student.

4. There is a need for clear district policy describing the primacy of language, i.e., the initial and continuing major instructional task is the development of language proficiency. The literature now supports quite strongly the concept that the critical variable related to achievement is proficiency of language, regardless of the particular language. Therefore, handicapped limited English proficient or bilingual students may very often have greater need for bilingual education ser-

vices than the "normal" LEP student. Since instruction and learning are dependent in our educational systems upon the development of language proficiency, attention must be devoted to the process of developing proficiency in the first language, and this proficiency should be demonstrated at a level appropriate for movement into academic learning in the second language.

5. School districts need explicit policies which require the monitoring of the language development process for the handicapped limited English proficient child. The information presented at the time of the original placement decision, Individual Educational Plan (IEP) development, and IEP revisions should include recent information relative to the language development progress of the child. Recognizing the primacy of language development to the educational processes, placement committees and those revising IEPs cannot make referral decisions without information on *current* language development status.

6. Districts should have explicit policies regarding the competencies of teachers serving bilingual limited English proficient handicapped students. Such competencies should be equal to those of teachers providing services to other children, i.e., the responsibility for instruction of the limited English proficient or bilingual handicapped student cannot be turned over to a bilingual aide. In fact, the district has an obligation, if the student is in need of ESL instruction or bilingual instruction, to have that instruction provided by teachers who are trained and competent.

7. District policy should explicitly delineate the exit criteria from special education for the limited English profi-

cient or bilingual handicapped student. These criteria should be identical to those for other handicapped students. That is, the student who is bilingual or limited English proficient and also handicapped should have the same criteria applied to exiting from special education as any other handicapped student.

8. Districts need a monitoring system to assure that district policies are being implemented as delineated and intended. The findings of this study indicated discrepancies in several areas between district special education policy and actual practice, especially in terms of the data to be gathered and the individuals involved in the referral, assessment and placement of bilingual handicapped students.

Professional Development

The implications for policy relative to professional development of staff are extensive when considered within the context of bilingual or limited English proficient handicapped students.

1. Based upon the current and emerging demography it becomes compelling for institutions of higher education providing pre-service training of regular educators, bilingual educators and special educators to have policies which require their training programs and skill development procedures to address the unique assessment, admission and instructional requirements of bilingual and limited English proficient handicapped students. Just as it has become appropriate to include those elements associated with special education programming within the pre-service training of regular education teachers, it should be equally rational for training programs to include information relative to

the bilingual or limited English proficient student and the interface between special education and bilingual education. Specialty training areas, such as those for school psychologists, educational diagnosticians, school counselors, etc., should include specific information associated with the unique service delivery needs of the limited English proficient or bilingual handicapped student.

2. There is a clear need for providing information and developing awareness and skills related to bilingual and limited English proficient handicapped students within a continuing education context. It is quite evident that the majority of educational service personnel are in place and will not be replaced by pre-service trained persons. Therefore, there should be policy requiring content related to serving bilingual and limited English proficient students to be included in in-service and continuing education activities for various professionals including administrators, assessment personnel and teachers.

The research literature supports the concept that for change and improvement to occur, there must be knowledge and support by key administrators such as the school principal. Therefore, school districts should have policies which assure that key administrators in all three complementary disciplines — special, bilingual and regular education do, in fact, have information and knowledge associated with providing appropriate services to limited English proficient and bilingual handicapped students.

Special education as a unit of the educational system is driven by the process of assessment to enter and exit special education. It behooves school districts to have policies which assure that assessment personnel have information, training and skills associated with the assessment of language, the assessment of handicaps and the assessment of academic learning competencies using appropriate procedures, instrumentation and interpretation for limited English proficient or bilingual handicapped students. Often, training at the continuing education level is not recognized as a need relative to school psychologists, diagnosticians, and counselors as they represent a relatively small percentage of the educational personnel. However, within the context of special education for this unique handicapped child, they become critical and must have appropriate information, knowledge and skills.

The need for teachers to have appropriate knowledge and skills relative to the limited English proficient or bilingual handicapped student is, of course, quite compelling. However, it must be made clear that districts should have policy stating that teachers in all three complementary disciplines — regular, special and bilingual education — have appropriate training to bring about the levels of understanding necessary to effectively serve this uniquely handicapped student. The literature from the effective schools research clearly points up the importance associated with teacher expectations. Such expectations for the limited English proficient bilingual student who is also handicapped must be addressed.

CONCLUSION

Current and emerging demography point to the critical need for education institutions to recognize and address the unique learning needs of bilingual and/or limited English proficient students. To ignore these needs reflects irresponsibility on the part of the educational system and of society, as in the future, society will be dependent upon the educational attainment of this minority population. Minority students, in fact, represent the "work force of this nation" for the next generation. Evidence from current practice within public schools confirms that there are, at this time, problems, difficulties, inefficiencies and inhumanity of service delivery to limited English proficient and bilingual handicapped students. These problems and difficulties must be addressed. There is a range of specific policies and procedures that school districts should feel obligated to implement or create in order to appropriately serve this unique handicapped student. To do less is, at best, poor educational practice, possibly and probably illegal, but most importantly, inhumane.

REFERENCES

Blaschke, C. L. (1979). *Case Study of the Implementation of Public Law 94-142*. Prepared for DHEW, Bureau of Education for the Handicapped (Contract No. 300-77-0528). Washington, D.C.: Educational Turnkey Systems, Inc.

Duncan, S. E., and DeAvila, E. (1981). *Scoring and Interpretation Manual for Language Assessment Scales* (LAS). San Rafael, CA: Linguametrics Group.

Dunn, L. M., and Markwardt, F. C., Jr. (1970). *Peabody Individual Assessment Test Manual.* Circle Pines, MN: American Guidance Service, Inc.

Garcia, S. B. (1984). *Effects of Student Characteristics, School Programs and Organization on Decision-making for the Placement of Hispanic Students in Classes for the Learning Disabled.* Unpublished doctoral dissertation, The University of Texas at Austin.

Feistritzer, C. E. (1985). *Cheating Our Children: Why We Need School Reform.* Washington, D.C.: National Center for Education Information.

Jastak, J. F., and Jastak, S. (1978). *The Wide Range Achievement Test: Manual of Instructions.* Wilmington, DE: Jastak Associates, Inc.

Koppitz, E. M. (1975). *The Bender Gestalt Test for Young Children (Vol. 2): Research and Application 1963-1973.* New York: Grune & Stratton.

Maldonado-Colon, E. (1984). *Profiles of Hispanic Students Placed in Speech, Hearing and Language Programs in a Selected School District in Texas.* Unpublished doctoral dissertation, University of Massachusetts.

McNett, I. (1983). *Demographic Imperatives: Implications for Educational Policy.* Washington, D.C.: American Council on Education, Forum of Educational Organization Leaders, Institute for Educational Leadership.

Mercer, J. R. (1973). *Labeling the Mentally Retarded: Clinical and Social System Perspectives on Mental Retardation.* Berkeley, CA: University of California Press.

Ortiz, A. A., and Yates, J. R. (1963). *Incidence of Exceptionality Among Hispanics: Implications for Manpower Planning. NABE JOURNAL,* 7(3), 41-53.

Shepard, L., and Smith, M. L. (1981). *Evaluation of the Identification of Perceptual-Communicative Disorders in Colorado.* Prepared under contract from the Colorado Department of Education. Boulder, CO: University of Colorado, Laboratory of Educational Research.

Stearns, M. S.; Green, D.; and David, J. L. (1980). *Local Implementation of Public Law 94-142: First Report of a Longitudinal Study.* Prepared for DHEW, Bureau of Education for the Handicapped (Contract No. 300-78-0030). Menlo Park, CA: SRI International.

Tucker, J. (1980). Ethnic proportions in classes for the learning disabled: Issues in non-biased assessment. *Journal of Special Education, 14*(1), 93-105.

Wechsler, D. (1974). *Manual for the Wechsler Intelligence Scale for Children—Revised.* New York: The Psychological Corporation.

There are hundreds of thousands of kids who can't understand English, so what are you going to do?

RICARDO MARTINEZ. Policy Analyst
Committee on Education and Jobs
U.S. House of Representatives

9

ISSUES IN THE IMPLEMENTATION OF MASTER'S LEVEL TRAINING PROGRAMS FOR BILINGUAL SPECIAL EDUCATION

Wayne H. Holtzman, Jr.

NEED FOR BILINGUAL EDUCATORS

There is an urgent need for trained bilingual personnel to serve Limited English Proficient (LEP) exceptional Hispanic students, especially in the state of Texas. A constant and ever growing stream of undocumented workers from Mexico, refugee families from Central America and a relatively high birth rate for Hispanics in the United States and abroad has resulted in a very large number of Hispanic children who are already enrolled or who are soon to enter our public schools. For example, while the 1982 Anglo student population in Texas schools shows a 5.7 percent drop when compared to data from 1972, the Hispanic student population increased by a significant 33.5 percent (Bynum, 1983). The numbers of Hispanic students should continue to mushroom at least during the next few years, so that sometime within the next fifteen years Texas public schools will be serving a "majority minority" population in which more than 50 percent of all students are either Hispanic or black. While exact figures are not available, a large proportion of these Hispanic students will be LEP and will come from families where Spanish is the dominant home language. Thus the current lack of trained bilingual teachers and educators should get even worse in the near future.

This situation becomes even more critical in the case of bilingual special education teachers because of the highly specialized level of expertise required to teach bilingual Hispanic children who are handicapped. Very few individuals have received the necessary training to become competent bilingual teachers of special education children, but the need for these teachers is great. Using Kaskowitz's (1977) incidence figures derived from national studies, Ortiz and Yates (1983) projected the number of Hispanic students that would be expected to be classified under the various handicapping conditions.

Table 1 shows that while the numbers of Hispanic students in different categories generally is less than would be expected, a disproportionately large number of Hispanics were classified as learning disabled (LD) students (315% more than was predicted). This trend continues to occur at an alarming rate (Texas Education Agency Fall Survey, 1983 and 1984), to the extent that even marginally qualified bilingual special education teachers are in very short supply.

REASONS WHY FEW INDIVIDUALS CHOOSE TO BECOME BILINGUAL SPECIAL EDUCATION TEACHERS

One would expect that a large number of individuals would be interested in receiving training in bilingual special education, given the current shortage in the state of Texas, but unfortunately this is not the case. There are numerous possible reasons why few individuals are entering the field of bilingual special education. The most important ones at the master's level are

TABLE 1
Summary of Special Education Service Incidence for Hispanics in Texas for 1981–1982

Type of Handicap	Kaskowitz' Traditionally Accepted Incidence	Expected No.* of Handicapped Hispanics	Total Being Served	% of Expected No. Being Served	Current Service Incidence
Visually Handicapped	.11	906	573	63%	.07
Hearing Impaired	54	8,237	1,277	16%	.16
Orthopedically Handicapped and Other	.43	3,542	3,170	89%	.38
Health Impaired, Mentally Retarded	1.80	14,828	8,734	59%	1.06
Emotionally Disturbed	1.60	13,180	3,659	28%	.44
Learning Disabled	2.00	16,476	51,942	315%	6.30
Speech Handicapped	3.20	26,360	19,363	73%	2.40

Note: These figures are based on the Texas Education Agency's Fall survey of general student population and the report of all special education students, including students contracted to approved non-public schools for 1981–1982. The Hispanic student population was 823, 775.

*These figures are based on Kaskowitz' 1977 traditional incidence figures.

briefly described below. Some, but not all of the following reasons are relevant for undergraduate and doctoral level training as well.

1. The number of Hispanics who complete studies at the undergraduate level is still quite small, and those who do graduate are not necessarily bilingual. Thus, the applicant pool is restricted.

2. Anglos and other non-Hispanics who are interested in the field often are unable to demonstrate a sufficient level of proficiency in Spanish.

3. Experienced teachers with bachelor's degrees often are limited in their ability to continue their education because of family and/or job obligations. The level of remuneration does not justify sacrificing one's job as well as that of a spouse to move a family to a new location. Since the vast majority of potential students are women, it is even more unlikely that their husbands would select to follow them in this endeavor.

4. Young people are choosing more lucrative fields such as business, engineering, and the hard sciences in which to pursue careers. The "do your own thing" mentality of the late 1960s and early 1970s has been replaced by a greater emphasis on relative economic rewards to be gained from specific career choices, with the career of education being near the bottom of the totem pole. The idealistic days of the Great Society may have been filled with unrealistic expectations, but the dedication and optimistic views of many teachers and other groups now are being transformed into bitterness and a sense of despair.

5. The "back to basics" movement has succeeded in

underlining the sad state of education in America's public schools, making it even less likely for qualified individuals to want to enter the field. The low status and low pay given teachers does not promote the teaching profession.

6. Abrupt and far-reaching changes in the Texas educational system are being implemented for the first time through passage of the controversial House Bill 72, resulting in many experienced teachers leaving the profession. An increasing amount of control is being placed on teachers who are forced to spend countless hours of their time on paperwork. Passing competency tests in basic content areas is being required of teachers in order to advance up the career ladder or even to maintain one's teaching position. In order to take education courses at the undergraduate level, students now must first pass a test of basic skills which was recently developed. Initial reports appear to indicate that of the Hispanics who take this test for the first time, between 60 percent and 80 percent of them fail, further depleting the pool of available bilingual education and bilingual special education teachers.

7. Increased tuition costs coupled with a gradual reduction in the commitment of the federal government to bilingual and special education training programs and to public education in general is making it more difficult for minority students to attend graduate school. It also is becoming more difficult to obtain federal grants to establish training programs and to provide stipends to deserving students. Most training programs seem to require at least four or five years of initial funding in order to recruit enough qualified students and faculty, and to plan and implement an

appropriate sequence of coursework. Oftentimes, two or three years of federal monies is not sufficient to meet this objective.

8. The lack of certification procedures in the area of bilingual special education in the United States means that teachers with no direct experience or training in bilingual special education are hired by school districts simply because they are bilingual. However, being bilingual does not in itself qualify an individual to teach bilingual exceptional children.

9. The perceptions shared by some Hispanics of the inflexible criteria used in evaluating graduate student applications discourages many potential students from applying to graduate programs, especially to large institutions. In reality, there exists a special admissions system in many state colleges and universities whereby academic departments can accept applicants to a program even though they do not meet the requirements of the Graduate School. However, few student applicants know of this procedure. For many of them, the fear of failing the Graduate Record Exam (GRE) is enough to cause them to refrain from applying to Graduate School. In addition, past accounts of alleged racial discrimination, whether true or not, may also contribute to a fear of being denied admission.

10. The current political climate in which the effectiveness of bilingual education programs has been severely questioned may tend to serve as a deterrent to individuals who are considering entering the fields of bilingual education or bilingual special education. The future of these fields is quite uncertain, and the ignorance of many key groups of individuals is widespread and deep-rooted regarding the value of bi-

lingualism, multicultural education, and programs for bilingual and LEP students with mild learning disabilities or other handicapping conditions. The extent of this ignorance (or downright aggression) towards these programs is shown by continued and projected reduced funding levels for the Office of Bilingual Education and Minority Language Affairs (OBEMLA). Lyons (1985) states that the Department of Education's justification for proposing to reduce training activities in bilingual education is due to "research findings which indicate that the demand for new bilingual education teachers is far less than previously believed."

TYPES OF BILINGUAL
SPECIAL EDUCATION
GRADUATE TRAINING PROGRAMS

Since bilingual special education is a new field of study, no precedent exists to indicate the appropriate academic department to which it should belong. Depending upon the university or college in question, a master's level bilingual special education training program might be found within a department of bilingual education, special education, curriculum and instruction, educational psychology, multicultural studies, or other. Additionally, the faculty hired to do the training will most assuredly not have had direct training in bilingual special education themselves because of the newness of the field. Their past programs of study vary considerably, but usually include psychology or various areas within the broad spectrum of education (i.e., special education, educational administration, bilingual education, educational psychology, etc.). This multi-faceted background of faculty can bring positive strengths and creativity to a new training program, although these same individuals are at a disadvantage in not having been trained specifically in bilingual special education. This point is critical, since without a high degree of expertise of faculty, the quality of training for teachers will not be adequate.

Orientations to training at the master's level vary somewhat from program to program. One commonly used procedure is to recruit former bilingual education teachers who subsequently obtain special education certification. These teachers happen to be bilingual but receive no formal training in bilingual special education. Instead, their coursework is similar or identical to that which is required of monolingual students who are pursuing degrees in special education. A second procedure used in other programs is to provide English as a Second Language (ESL) or bilingual education certification to individuals who have had past training in the area of special education. Not all of these individuals need be bilingual. Depending upon the specific type of training program and experience of the faculty guiding the program, an emphasis in either bilingual education or special education concepts usually occurs, but rarely does a program attempt to integrate both bilingual education and special education constructs into a separate field of study.

One training program that promotes an integrated approach to the study of bilingual special education is at the University of Texas at Austin. Here, it is not sufficient to be bilingual. Instead, graduates should be able to provide appropriate instruction for bilingual and/or LEP Hispanic children through an integrated knowledge base which includes tenets of both bilingual education and special education. This view closely follows many of the ideas that Baca (1984) proposed when speaking about a bilingual special education "interface." Other features of the master's level training program at this institution require that students be bilingual, since they will need to use these abilities when they return to the classroom or to other positions within a school district. Bilingual faculty should be qualified to teach one or more courses in Spanish, since many of the assessment instruments and curricular materials which bilingual special education personnel use are in Spanish. Although it is better to have full-time students in a given training program, courses are offered in the late afternoon and evening so that students who are employed full-time as teachers can pursue the master's degree on a part-time basis.

In summary, the creation and implementation of highly specialized innovative bilingual special education training programs in the state of Texas and throughout the nation has been and will continue to be a real challenge for the program directors and faculty involved. Although there are obstacles which may tend to suppress the effective implementation of these programs, the need for qualified bilingual professionals in bilingual education and bilingual special education will continue to grow at an increasingly alarming rate. Graduates of these training programs will be pleased to find that many jobs exist in different areas of the country, with large urban school districts often offering very attractive economic incentives to trained bilingual teachers. Having obtained a master's degree in bilingual special education should definitely aid in promoting these individuals up a successful career ladder.

REFERENCES

Baca, L. M., and Cervantes, H. T. (1984). *The Bilingual Special Education Interface.* St. Louis, MO: Times Mirror/Mosby College Publishing Company.

Bynum, R. (1983). *Who Will Teach? What Do We Teach? Who Will Pay?* Paper presented at the meeting of the School Administrators Advisory Conference on Education, Austin, Texas.

Kaskowitz, D. H. (1977). *Validation of State Counts of Handicapped Children. Estimation of the Number of Handicapped Children in Each State.* Menlo Park, CA: Stanford Research Institute.

Lyons, J. J. (1985). The Reagan administration's FY 1986 budget for OBEMLA. *NABE News, 8*(3), p. 6.

Ortiz, A., and Yates, J. (1983). Incidence of exceptionality among Hispanics: Implications for manpower planning. *Journal of the National Association for Bilingual Education, 6*(3), pp. 41-53.

Texas Education Agency (1983, 1984). *Fall Survey of Handicapped Students in Texas Public Schools.* Austin, TX: Texas Education Agency.

I find when the non-English-speaking children aren't segregated, when they're treated the same as the English speakers, they learn and assimilate much more quickly.

DORIS ROWE, teacher

10

EXAMINING ASSUMPTIONS AND INSTRUCTIONAL PRACTICES RELATED TO THE ACQUISITION OF LITERACY WITH BILINGUAL SPECIAL EDUCATION STUDENTS

Barbara Flores, Robert Rueda, and Brenda Porter

INTRODUCTION

One of the more common academic difficulties experienced by mildly handicapped students is the acquisition of acceptable levels of literacy skills. Although this topic has occupied the attention of both researchers and practitioners, the issue has become more complex with the increasing amount of attention focused on those special education students with limited skills in English (Baca and Cervantes, 1984; Omark and Erickson, 1983). The increasing numbers of such students, especially in large urban school districts, have hastened the search for effective instructional practices to assure future participation in literate society. In this article, we briefly examine the theoretical model and assumptions of traditional instructional practices which have been used with monolingual special education students. Further, we consider the development of an alternative model based upon recent theoretical developments, and discuss the application with LEP special education students acquiring English writing skills.

A TRADITIONAL APPROACH
TO THE DEVELOPMENT OF LITERACY

Traditionally, special education students have been taught basic literacy skills (reading and writing) from a part to whole perspective. This instructional model is guided by commonly held assumptions about language and literacy development. Under this model, it is assumed that lower order, basic literacy skills must be mastered as a prerequisite to the development of higher order literacy skills. In the area of reading, for example, it is believed that learning is best accomplished by instructing from the simple to the complex. That is, children must first learn the sounds, the letter-sound correspondence, and word recognition skills. This is followed by reading simple sentences, and finally by reading vocabulary controlled stories in basal readers. It is common instructional practice to teach reading in this sequential order, assuming that teaching in this order is how students will best learn. Writing is also assumed to be learned in a sequential, hierarchical order as well. Students are commonly taught to form the letters through practice first, then to copy words and sentences. Additionally, they are required to fill in workbook pages with specific skills related to writing that generally focus on rules about correct grammar usage, correct punctuation, and spelling. In other words, it is assumed that by teaching the rules about written language usage, correct standard conventions will be acquired.

Although the hierarchical and sequential aspects of the traditional model are important, another widely held assumption is that literacy (including both reading and writing) must be error free. Errors are categorically dismissed as an indication that students are not learning. Students are expected to perform accurately as a demonstration that learning is occurring. The conceptualization of reading and writing embodied in this last assumption is that reading and writing are exact and precise processes. Harste and Burke (1977) have suggested that instruction based upon the assumption of the traditional model just reviewed reflects a "skills" view of language and literacy learning and teaching.

A RECONSIDERATION BASED UPON THEORETICAL ADVANCES

Although the preceding "skills" model is most commonly used to guide instructional practice in the development of literacy, recent theoretical advances in various fields suggest that the teaching of literacy may need to be reconceptualized. While it may be true that a sequential, hierarchically ordered approach which breaks a task into small steps is effective for teaching discrete skills, there is a certain danger involved. As Riel (1983) says:

> The weakness is that learners are so thoroughly guided through the small pieces of the task that they may lose sight of what they are trying to do. The danger is that they will learn that learning is simply repeating the steps that the teacher provides. By breaking the task down into small tasks, it leaves the students the difficult task of reassembling the pieces to make sense of the whole activity. It also frequently ignores the goal structures of the learner by trying to supplant them with the goals of the learner (1983, p. 60).

Recent work on the socio-historical approach to cognitive development (Vygotsky 1978; Wertsch, Minick and Arns, 1984; Moll, Estrada, Diaz, and Lopes, 1980; Scribner and Cole), and in the areas of psycholinguistics (Goodman, 1965, 1967, 1969, 1970, 1979; Goodman and Burke, 1968, 1969, 1973; Goodman and Goodman, 1977, 1978, 1981; Goodman, 1984; Smith, 1975, 1982; Harste, Woodward and Burke, 1984; Edelsky, et al., 1981, 1983, 1985; and Haussler, 1984), and sociolinguistics (Halliday, 1973, 1975, 1978) raise important questions about instructional practices governed by the assumptions of the traditional "skills" model. These theoretical frameworks suggest a more holistic approach to the conceptualization and instruction of literacy as a social, functionally embedded activity. More specifically, the guiding assumptions can be summarized as follows: (1) language and literacy (either in L1 or in L2) are best learned when presented in authentic situations reflecting real needs, purposes, and functions (Halliday, 1973); (2) language and literacy represent transactive processes (Rosenblatt, 1978) that focus on the construction of meaning (Goodman, 1967); (3) control of the form (i.e., the mechanics) is best learned in the context of its authentic use (function, purpose, need); (4) the teacher promotes the development of language and literacy by deliberately creating a social context in which they form a central part of the activity; and (5) social interaction between "novices" and "experts" in the "zone of proximal development" is the primary mechanism which drives the process of learning (Vygotsky, 1978).

FROM THEORY TO PRACTICE

Rueda, Flores and Porter (1986, elsewhere in this book) have recently reported on an ethnographic study of a mildly handicapped special education classroom in which bilingual (and in some cases trilingual) students were exposed to "holistically" based writing experiences reflecting the preceding assumptions. The teacher, who formed a part of the research team, had shifted from a primarily "skills" based framework to a more holistic model emphasizing the teaching of reading and writing as functional, useful skills embedded in authentic social contexts. Building upon the previous work of the first author (Flores and Garcia, 1984), the research team began to explore ways to incorporate the developing theoretical framework into everyday practice. The primary results of this collaborative work was the introduction of interactive journal writing as a regular part of the classroom experience. (See Rueda, Flores and Porter, 1985 in press, for a more detailed description of the classroom).[1]

Staton (1980, 1983) has referred to teacher-student written correspondence as "dialogue journals." We (Flores, et al., 1985; Flores and Garcia, 1984) prefer the term "interactive journals" since it more closely reflects the theoretical notions which have guided its use in this classroom. Through the use of interactive journal writing, student-teacher communication is distributed across time and across space. Most importantly,

---

[1]The purpose of the intervention in this classroom was not bilingual instruction per se. In fact, because of their special education placements, district policy did not permit eligibility for ESL placement for these students. Rather, we were interested in developing higher order literacy skills (communication of meaning in creative, authentic ways).

however, interactive journal writing represents an authentic, social communicative event using written language. Both participants engage in authentic exchanges by focusing on meaningful and purposeful communication, with the main goal communicating feelings and thoughts. Writing mechanics and correct spelling are not considerations in the teacher's response to students. Rather, "errors" are seen as a necessary part of learning and development. Although "correct" spelling and writing skills are modeled in the response of the teacher, thus creating a "zone of proximal development," the primary goal remains the communication of meaning in authentic interaction.

Our initial experiences in this classroom demonstrated that if neither the student nor the teacher engage in authentic exchanges, the result would most likely be contrite, mundane writing. This was especially true in those instances where students were required to complete endless, written drill sheets focused on small, discrete subskills deemed necessary for "correct" writing. However, if the students are able to internalize the realization that the teacher is really interested in what the student has to say and also shares his/her life experiences, feelings, ideas, attitudes, values and beliefs, then the teacher and student quickly move toward the intended purpose of the activity and begin to engage in a mutually defined and constructed authentic literacy event.[2]

The teacher's decision to shift to a more holistic paradigm was both deliberate and difficult. For example, in interactive journal writing the focus is the authentic use of written lan-

[2]Note the similarity between this approach to teach facility with writing language and Krashen's (1981, 1982) approach to second language acquisition.

guage and not the productive use of standard ("correct") writing conventions. Our theoretical framework suggested that allowing students to take risks in using written language without focusing first on the "correct" form would promote the students' (novices) control of the mechanics and other subskills in the context of their exposure to the teacher's (the expert) written response. However, it became apparent that students had internalized the purpose of writing as proficiency with mechanical skills. More importantly, the teacher initially felt uncomfortable not correcting "errors."

In spite of these problems, the teacher was dissatisfied with the students' progress in language and literacy under a "skills" model. Year after year she taught the same skills. Yet year after year the students still "didn't get it." "How can that be?" she often queried. Perhaps it was the assumptions guiding the way that she was teaching. These lingering questions and her need for an increased understanding of how children learn language and literacy prompted a collaborative journey with the first two authors.

To date, our preliminary analysis of some of the bilingual special education students' journal entries across a whole year support the theoretical premises guiding intervention in the classroom. Figure 1 demonstrates the manner in which an eleven-year-old trilingual (English, Spanish, Yaqui) fifth grade learning disabled student attempts to communicate both excitement and inquisitiveness about an out of school event with his teacher. This particular student had recorded scores at the following grade levels on the California Achievement Test: grammar, 2.5; written expression, 1.9; total, 2.7. The teacher's response to his journal entry is shown in Fig. 2.

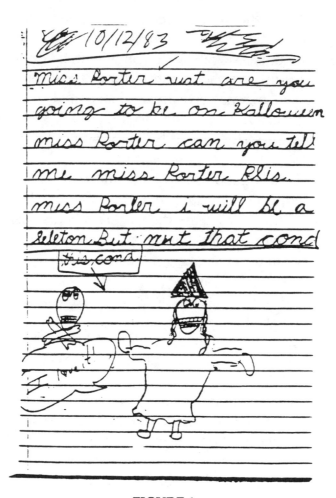

FIGURE 1

Translation: Miss Porter what are you going to be on Halloween? Miss Porter, can you tell me? Miss Porter, Please. Miss Porter, I will be a skeleton. But not that kind. This kind.

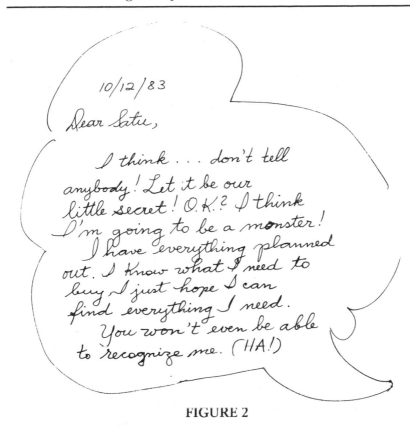

FIGURE 2

Ms. Porter's authentic response to Satu's request shows her deliberate enthusiasm and genuine interest. By example she demonstrates authentic communication.

Traditionally, from a "skills" perspective, Satu's writing would be diagnosed as an example of a learning disability. However, from a developmental, holistic perspective, several strengths are evident. Santo has internalized the intent of authenticity in this literacy event. Further, he demonstrates a knowledge of the capitalization of proper nouns and the beginning of sentences. He appears to realize that it is acceptable to use

157

invented spellings to communicate his message until he is able to master the standard orthography. No, it is not the case that he is learning bad habits. Yes, he needs to acquire standard usage of punctuation and spelling, and he does. In fact, his use of conventional spelling increased dramatically throughout the year.

However, the acquisition occurs naturally while embedded in a larger, meaningful whole activity, and is subordinate to the goal of "making sense." These observations correspond to Halliday's notion that form generally follows function (Halliday, 1975).

Another interesting characteristic of this student's writing sample is that he is practicing the use of a cursive writing style. This is significant in light of the fact that the teacher had not formally taught the students to write in cursive. Yet, as the teacher's response demonstrates, she uses standard conventions. In this respect, she is acting as a scaffold (Wood, Burner and Ross, 1976). In her responses, the teacher is deliberately yet naturally providing adult guidance to the "novice" writer in an authentic social context. As Greenfield (1984) has suggested:

> The scaffold, as it is known in building construction, has five characteristics: it provides a support; it functions as a tool; it extends the range of the worker; it allows the worker to accomplish a task not otherwise possible; and it is used selectively to aid the worker where needed . . . the teacher's selective intervention provides a supportive tool for the learner, which extends his or her skills, thereby allowing the learner successfully to accomplish a task not otherwise possible. (p. 118)

A similar view of the learning process has been elaborated by Vygotsky (1978) in the form of the zone of proximal development. This is described as " . . . the distance between the actual developmental level as determined by independent problem solving and the level of potential development as determined through problem solving under adult guidance or in collaboration with more capable peers . . . the zone of proximal development defines those functions that have not yet matured but are in the process of maturation, functions that will mature tomorrow, but are currently in an embryonic state." (p. 86)

Further elaboration of the manner in which these "assisted interactions" are incorporated into writing events are demonstrated in the following examples. Two weeks later, Santo's journal reflects some standard writing mechanics which were previously used inconsistently (Fig. 3).

The fluency and voice of the message convey the "spookiness" that he wants to create. His use of standard spelling has approximated standard form 48 times out of 61. In other words, he appropriately used conventional spelling approximately eighty percent of the time in spontaneous writing. In addition, he has incorporated the use of exclamation marks which the teacher had used two weeks earlier. Although appropriate ending punctuation is not being consistently demonstrated, its use is in a developing, transitional stage.

Figure 4 reflects in detail a close correspondence with his written message, and it reinforces the communicative intent of the writing activity.

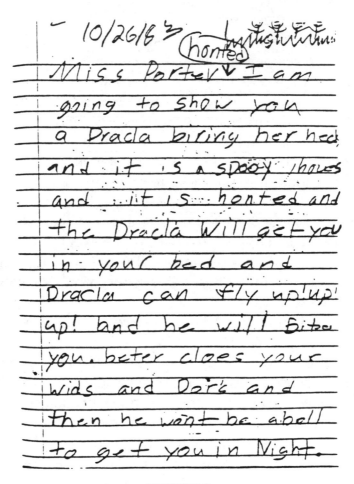

FIGURE 3

Translation: Miss Porter I am going to show you a Dracula biting her neck and it is a spooky house and it is haunted and the Dracula will get you in your bed and Dracula can fly up! up! up! And he will bite you. Better close your windows and doors and then he won't be able to get you in (the) night.

160

FIGURE 4

CONCLUSION

The brief example presented is meant to exemplify the collaborative attempt to apply the theoretical framework described in an actual learning context. It is fair to predict that without intervention, the student whose writing sample was presented would have acquired only minimal literacy skills, as would the other students in the classroom where this approach has been implemented. Our initial experiences suggest that these bilingual and trilingual special education students, whose past school careers have certainly been problematic, are learning, developing, and evolving in the use of language and literacy through the use of carefully and systematically constructed authentic literacy events.

161

The example further demonstrates how the teacher provides "assisting interactions" and serves as a scaffold in providing adult guidance, in effect creating a zone of proximal development for the developing literacy skills of the students. The theoretical considerations outlined, as well as the short example highlighted here, raise serious questions about traditional "skill-based" instructional practices that teach literacy "skills" in isolation with little regard to the functional, culturally constructed contexts in which those skills will eventually be required. In addition, the preceding discussion demonstrates one potentially effective approach to facilitating the acquisition of literacy in a second language in those special cases where traditional approaches have resulted in limited success.

REFERENCES

Bacca, L., and Cervantes, H. (1984). *The Bilingual Special Education Interface*. St. Louis, MO: Times Mirror/Mosby College Publishing.

Edelsky, C. (1981). From "Jimosalsco" to "7 narangas se calleron y el arbolest-triste en lagrymas": Writing development in a bilingual program. In B. Cronnell (Ed.), *The Writing Needs of Linguistically Different Students*. Los Alamitos, CA: Southwest Regional Laboratory.

Edelsky, C., Draper, K., and Smith, K. (1983). Hookin' 'em in at the start of school in a "Whole Language" classroom. *Anthropology and Education Quarterly*, 14(4), 257-281.

Edelsky, C. (1985). *Writing in a Bilingual Program: Habia una vez*. Norwood, NJ: Ablex. (in press).

Flores, B., and Garcia, E. (1984). A collaborative learning and teaching experience using journal writing. *Journal of the National Association of Bilingual Education*, 8(2), 67-83.

Flores, B., Garcia, E., Gonzalez, S., Hidalgo, G., Kaczmarek, K., and Romero, T. (1985). *Bilingual Holistic Instructional Strategies*. Phoenix, AZ: Exito, Inc.

Goodman, K. S. (1965). A linguistic study of cues and miscues in reading. *Elementary English,* 42, 639-643.

Goodman, K. S. (1967). Reading: A psycholinguistic guessing game. *Journal of the Reading Specialist,* 4, 126-135.

Goodman, K. S. (1969). Dialect barriers to reading comprehension. In J. C. Baratz and R. W. Shuy (Eds.), *Teaching Black Children to Read.* Washington, D.C.: Center for Applied Linguistics.

Goodman, K. S. (1970). Psycholinguistic universals in the reading process. *Typographic Research,* Spring, 103-110.

Goodman, K. S. (1979). The know-more and know-nothing movements in reading: A personal response. *Language Arts,* September, 658-663.

Goodman, K. S., and Burke, C. L. (1968). *Study of Children's Behavior While Reading Orally.* Final Report Project No. S425, Contract No. OE-6-10-136. United States Department of Health, Education and Welfare, Office of Education.

Goodman, K. S., and Burke, C. L. (1969). *Study of Oral Reading Miscues that Result in Grammatical Retransforation.* Final Report Project No. 7-E-219, Contract No. OE-6-0-8-070219-2806 (010), United States Department of Health, Education and Welfare, Office of Education.

Goodman, K. S., and Burke, C. L. (1973). *Theoretically Based Studies of Patterns of Miscues in Oral Reading Performance.* Final Report Project No. 90375, Grant No. OE-0-9-320375-4269, United States Department of Health, Education and Welfare, Office of Education.

Goodman, K. S., and Goodman, Y. M. (1977). Learning about psycholinguistic processes by analyzing oral reading. *Harvard Educational Review,* 47(3), 317-333.

Goodman, K. S., and Goodman, Y. M. (1978). *Reading of American Children Whose Language is a Stable Rural Dialect of English or a Language Other than English.* Final Report, Project NIE-C-OD-300087. Washington, D.C.: National Institute of Education.

Goodman, K. S., and Goodman, Y. M. (1981). A whole-language comprehension centered view of reading development. Tucson, AZ: Arizona Center for Research and Development, University of Arizona.

Goodman, Y. (1980). *The Roots of Literacy.* Claremont, CA: Claremont Reading Conference Forty-fourth Yearbook.

Greenfield, P. M. (1984). A theory of the teacher in the learning activities of everyday life. In B. Rogoff and J. Lave (Eds.), *Everyday Cognition: Its Development in Social Context.* Cambridge, MA: Harvard University Press.

Halliday, M. A. K. (1973). *Explorations in the Functions of Language.* London: Edward Arnold (Publishers) Ltd.

Halliday, M. A. K. (1975). *Learning How to Mean: Explorations in the Development of Language.* London: Edward Arnold (Publishers) Ltd.

Halliday, M. A. K. (1978). *Language as Social Semiotic: The Social Interpretation of Language and Meaning.* London: Edward Arnold (Publishers) Ltd.

Harste, J., and Burke, C. L. (1977). A new hypotheses for reading teacher research: Both teaching and learning of reading are theoretically based. In P. D. Pearson (Ed.), *Reading: Theory, Research and Practice.* Twenty-sixth Yearbook of the National Reading Conference. St. Paul, MN: Mason Publishing Co.

Harste, J., Woodard, V., and Burke, C. L. (1984). *Language Stories and Literacy Lessons.* Portsmouth, NH: Heinemann Educational Books.

Haussler, M. (1984). *Transitions Into Literacy: A Working Paper.* Tucson, AZ: Arizona Center for Research and Development, University of Arizona.

Krashen, S. D. (1981). Bilingual education and second language acquisition theory. In California State Department of Education, *Schooling and Language Minority Students: A Theoretical Framework.* Los Angeles, CA: Evaluation, Dissemination and Assessment Center.

Krashen, S. D. (1982). *Principles and Practice in Second Language Acquisition.* Oxford: Pergammon Press.

Moll, L. C., Estrada, E., Diaz, E., and Lopez, L. The organization of bilingual lessons: Implications for schooling. *L.C.H.C. Newsletter,* July 1980, 2(3), 53–58.

Omark, D. R., and Erickson, J. G. (Eds.) (1983). *The Bilingual Exceptional Child.* San Diego, CA: College-Hill Press.

Riel, M. (1983). Education and ecstacy: Computer chronicles of students writing together. *The Quarterly Newsletter of the Laboratory of Comparative Human Cognition,* 5(3), 59–67.

Rosenblatt, L. (1978). *The Reader, the Text, and the Poem.* Carbondale, IL: Illinois University Press.

Rueda, R., Flores, B., and Porter B. (1985). Aspects of literacy and social interaction in a special education classroom with bilingual students. In E. Garcia and B. Flores (Eds.), *Advances in Bilingual Education Research: Language and*

Literacy Development, Volume II. Tempe, AZ: Arizona State University Press (in press).

Scritner, S., and Cole M. (1981). *The Psychology of Literacy.* Cambridge: Harvard University Press.

Smith, F. (1975). *Understanding Reading.* New York, NY: Holt, Rinehart & Winston.

Smith, F. (1978). *Reading Without Nonsense.* New York, NY: Teachers College Press.

Stanton, J. (1980). Writing and counseling: Using a dialogue journal. *Language Arts,* 57, 514-518.

Stanton, J. (1983). Dialogue journals: A new tool for teaching communication. *ERIC/DLL NewsBulletin,* 6, 1-2; 6.

Vygotsky, L. S. (1978). *Mind in Society: The Development of Higher Psychological Processes.* Cambridge: Harvard University Press.

Wertsch, J. V., Minick, N., and Arns, F. J. (1984). The creation of context in joint problem-solving. In B. Rogoff and J. Lave (Eds.), *Everyday Cognition: Its Development in Social Context.* Cambridge, MA: Harvard University Press.

Wood, D., Bruner, J. S., and Ross, G. (1976). The role of tutoring in problem-solving. *Journal of Child Psychology and Psychiatry,* 17, 89-100.

Those children who did not do well were those who arrived at school with low language and prereading skills to begin with, not whether they spoke Spanish or English. And without sufficient special assistance in their native language they don't do well in the later grades.

BETTY J. MACE-MATLUCK
Southwest Educational Development Laboratory

11

LANGUAGE, LITERACY, AND INSTRUCTION IN BILINGUAL SETTINGS:

Issues and Implications of Findings from a Recent Longitudinal Study

Betty J. Mace-Matluck and Wesley A. Hoover

Each year the number of Hispanic children enrolled in the nation's schools increases. In Texas, about a third of the school children are from Spanish language backgrounds, with half of the current kindergarten population Hispanic. A similar pattern of growth is repeated in all of the US–Mexico border states and, to a lesser extent, throughout the country.

Implications for the social, economic, and political future of the United States are clear. If these children fail to learn and achieve in school, the nation loses a vast resource, and risks, in the next generation, disaffection and economic and social alienation.

Generally, children from Spanish language backgrounds, for many reasons, encounter difficulty in our nation's schools. It is well documented that these children do more poorly than the general school population on standardized achievement tests and their dropout rate is higher.

However, the Hispanic population is far from homogeneous. Differences within the group include degree of bilingualism, length of family residence in the United States (immigrant versus long-term settlement), country or region of origin, socio-economic conditions, mobility, ways in which English and

Spanish are used in the various domains of life and thought, and experience with print both in and out of school.

THE STUDY

Given the circumstances cited above and the startling lack of solid evidence about which approaches or combination of approaches are most effective in teaching Hispanic children, the National Institute of Education contracted with the Southwest Educational Development Laboratory (SEDL) to conduct a comprehensive, six-year longitudinal investigation covering the primary grades. The study, conducted in Texas, was designed to examine the relations between current schooling practices and the language and reading achievement of some 250 Spanish-speaking children from low-income Hispanic families who began their initial schooling in transitional bilingual education programs. The study sought to provide information that could give greater insights into (a) what constitutes a favorable learning environment for children from Spanish-language backgrounds, (b) what instructional sequences and events promote successful and efficient learning of literacy skills, and (c) what the language and literacy outcomes of current schooling practices are for these youngsters.

To meet the objectives of the study, the students' entry skills and subsequent achievement in oral language and the various components of reading were assessed yearly from kindergarten through fourth grade. Systematic observation was carried out in each classroom; information was gathered about the teachers' instructional plans; and the nature of each instructional program was documented. Finally, the students' rates and patterns of growth in literacy were investigated in relation to the instruction received.

The data revealed that the students, on average, were acquiring oral language skills at the rate expected (based on the difficulty level of the test materials) and were gaining in English literacy at or near a year of gain for a year of instruction. Slightly more than half of the students were reading in English at grade-level expectations by the end of second grade. It was projected that by the end of fourth grade the overall sample of students would score within a grade level of expectation on performance-based reading tests, with students who entered with relatively higher English skills scoring slightly above grade-level expectations. Strongly related to reading achievement in each grade level (first through fourth) were kindergarten entry language skills, performance during the previous year, and the quantity and quality of the reading instruction. The data suggest that the transitional bilingual programs studied are promoting English literacy for all students, but without strong support from the home, school, and community, the students in these programs are not likely to achieve high levels of literacy in Spanish.

During the course of the investigation, a number of critically important instructional issues surrounding language and literacy growth were identified. These issues and their related implications as manifested in the findings from the study are examined below.

ISSUES AND IMPLICATIONS OF THE FINDINGS

Valid Language Assessment

Issue. What constitutes a valid assessment of oral proficiency? Analyses of the study's oral language data (teacher ratings, oral language proficiency tests, and free-speech samples) suggest that none of the measures by themselves provides adequate information. When taken in combination, however, the data provided by different types of measures and procedures can provide a reasonably accurate index of oral abilities.

Implications. Given that results of oral language assessment figure prominently in a number of educational decisions for language minority children (e.g., identification, program placement, termination of special services), further research is needed to determine not only *effective,* but *practical* means for assessing such proficiency (e.g., observation of student functional use of language by trained teacher observers).

Language and Instructional Program

Issue. To what extent does the child's language at school entry determine nominal program placement, and once assigned to a program, the actual instruction delivered? By legislative mandate, all children in Texas from non-English language backgrounds, who, at school entry, score below a predetermined score in English, are placed in a bilingual education program. This placement implies some use of the home language for instruction for some given period of time.

Implications. Given the suggestion that multiple measures are needed to obtain valid assessments of proficiency, school districts should be discouraged from relying on a single source of information for placement decisions. Further, given that teacher perception of student language ability determines, to a large extent, the instructional treatment delivered within the classroom (i.e., the use of the home language both as a medium of instruction and for support within the classroom), teachers should be knowledgeable about and have significant input into the oral language assessment process, particularly as related to entry/exit decisions. Teacher training for assessing oral language should focus on both how to observe language behavior and what to observe (e.g., social, personal, and cognitive aspects of oral proficiency in addition to linguistic dimensions).

Language Development and Reading Acquisition

Issue. To what extent does the child's language development at the time of school entry affect subsequent reading achievement? The literature includes numerous studies showing moderate to strong relationships between oral language development and reading achievement (Clarke, 1981; Cziko, 1980; Goldman, Reyes, & Varnhagen, 1984; Goodman & Goodman, 1978; Matluck & Mace-Matluck, 1981; Tregar, Brisk, Indresano, & Lombardo, 1981). To learn to read, children must bring their knowledge of spoken language to written language. A well-developed system of oral language assumes a functional vocabulary and the ability to discover the structure and meaning of spoken utterances. It also assumes a certain ability to reflect upon language in ways which allow the discovery of the properties of spoken language that are central to the correspondence between its written and spoken forms. Children who do not have a well-developed understanding of the communicative process at school entry often experience difficulties in learning to read, and therefore fall below the school's academic expectations. In the SEDL study, teachers rated the entry oral language skills of approximately 25% of the students as relatively low in both languages.

Implications.   School-based preschool programs and parent involvement components of school programs have gained support as means of enhancing the language development of young children. With adequate attention to staff development, instructional focus, monitoring, and funding, such programs could significantly advance the language development of "high risk" youngsters and should therefore be made more widely available to low-income language minority students. Similarly, refined oral language instruction that focuses on school-related discourse in the early grades could advance the students readiness for academic work.

Pre-reading Skills and Reading Achievement

Issue.   To what extent does the child's pre-reading skills development at entry affect subsequent reading achievement? When compared with children with less well-developed skills at entry, children with relatively better developed pre-reading skills (e.g., verbal skills, phonemic awareness, knowledge of the alphabet) at entry were better able to take advantage of the instruction offered and to maintain their relatively superior level of attainment in reading throughout the primary grades.

Those children with less well-developed skills often become

locked into an instructional track in which the instruction is the same as for other students, only at a slower pace. Such instruction provides these students with opportunities to learn only a narrow range of the skills and content needed to become fluent readers.

Implications. A challenge for the schools is to find means to help prepare the less academically advantaged children to benefit from instruction and to accelerate their growth in the early years so they can keep up with their age group in the general school population. As discussed above, well-designed oral language instruction in the early grades, as well as pre-school programs, could expand the knowledge and experience base needed for subsequent academic learning. Further, the whole concept of ability grouping for instruction and instructional "tracking" needs to be closely scrutinized, as such organizational procedures may not be in the best interest of low achieving students.

Rate and Pattern of Language and Reading Growth

Issue. To what extent does growth and development of oral language *following* school entry contribute to reading achievement? Most children by the age of five have control of the basic structure of their native language and of most of the complexities of conversational interaction. However, when they enter school, children confront a new speech environment with different linguistic requirements for accomplishing informational and social goals. Students from non-English backgrounds must not only master the grammar of a new language, but many must also learn to communicate in the unique setting of the classroom.

Although there is no significant "transition" involving grammar, phonology, or even vocabulary in a given language between that required for communicating in the home ("natural language") and the school ("formal language"), differences do occur in the nature of the interactions (Klee, 1984; Mehan, 1979; Wells, 1983). For example, the relative frequency of certain types of interaction differ (more question-answer sequences in the classroom and more pseudo-questions where the asker already knows the answer); the role of the participants differs (in the classroom, the teacher most often initiates the topic and assumes the authority role while the student acts as recipient); and the conversational structure of classroom talk differs (the child must learn how to engage the teacher and others to acquire the necessary input for learning, and when and under what conditions a turn can be negotiated).

A number of scholars (Bruner, 1975; Cummins, 1981; Donaldson, 1978; Olson, 1977; Calfee & Freedman, 1980; Swain, 1981) describe differences in the use and interpretation of language in face-to-face communication and language used autonomously. In the former, the language is supported by contextual and paralinguistic cues, and, therefore, is less dependent on the specific linguistic forms used for its interpretation than on the expectation and perception of the speaker's intentions and the salient features of the context. In contrast, language that moves beyond the bounds of interpersonal context makes different demands on the individual and requires the user to focus on the linguistic forms themselves for meaning, since meaning is autonomously represented and contextual support is greatly reduced. The linguistic message must, therefore, be elaborated precisely and explicitly, whether in oral or written form.

To a considerable extent, formal education teaches the child to process and produce formal spoken and written language. In acquiring literacy, children learn to assign meaning to the linguistic forms per se, and they become conscious of the process by which language can be controlled and manipulated to gain knowledge and to apply that knowledge in a variety of academic and social contexts. Learning to deal with language in this manner is necessary for reading success, yet for many, it is difficult to acquire.

The SEDL sample of children developed oral English skills at a rate which exceeded the expectations of a year of growth for a year of instruction. The students made considerable progress not only in learning English grammar, but also in acquiring the dimensions of formal language. Their oral Spanish skills, in contrast, proceeded at only half the expected rate and were projected to fall below grade-level expectations during the primary grades. The lesser growth in oral Spanish skills can be explained in part by the fact that only a third of the sample received literacy instruction in Spanish in the early grades. Nonetheless, mastery of a second language beyond that required for interpersonal communication takes time. Even with the considerable emphasis on English reading instruction, the English oral skills of those students with relatively low English skills at entry (while showing greater growth rates in such skill), did not converge with those students who had relatively higher English skills at entry until late fourth grade.

Entry oral language skills were related to both decoding skills and reading comprehension. Students who entered with relatively higher oral skills in a given language tended to show greater skill in decoding in that language than did students with lower oral skills. However, on average, the total sample of students learned to decode words in isolation in both languages at rates exceeding expectation and were above grade-level expectation in decoding throughout the primary grades. In contrast their reading *rate* (i.e., decoding fluency) was slow in both languages (less than two syllables per second by the end of second grade).

Oral language entry skills also were substantially related to performance in reading comprehension. Students who entered with relatively high English oral skills also entered with better developed reading comprehension skills. While growth rates did not differ for the two groups, the entry advantage of those with relatively higher oral skills resulted in consistently higher levels of achievement in reading comprehension. Furthermore, children who entered with relatively higher *Spanish* oral skills had growth rates in *English* reading comprehension exceeding those of students who entered with less well developed skills in Spanish. These findings suggest that children who come to school with well developed oral language skills in *either* or *both* languages have an advantage in learning to read connected text.

Implications. Effective means for increasing decoding fluency need to be identified and communicated to teachers, as low fluency may be impeding reading growth.

Some students in the study were deemed by their teachers to have had relatively low oral language skills in both Spanish and English on entry into school. Since entry oral language skills were found to be associated with reading performance, research that can assist schools in working effectively with such students appears to be warranted.

Transfer of Skills Across Languages

Issue. To what extent do knowledge and skills gained in one language transfer to similar tasks in another known language? An underlying premise of transitional bilingual education is that reading skills gained in initial instruction in the home language can be transferred to reading in English and that children, having learned to read successfully in their home language, can be taught to read at the same level in English rather quickly, once oral English skills have reached an acceptable proficiency level.

In the SEDL study, the correlation patterns between the English and Spanish reading measures suggest that a child's knowledge and skills associated with decoding are related across the two languages, as are those associated with overall reading ability (but to a lesser degree). This finding supports the notion that reading knowledge and skills gained in one language can be transferred to reading in another known language.

Implications. The practice of teaching children to read initially in their stronger language appears to be educationally sound. However, in commenting on the transfer of learning within a bilingual setting, researchers (e.g., Moll, Díaz, Estrada, & Lopes, 1981) contend that learning is primarily situation specific; generalizing to other situations depends upon organizing the environment to facilitate application to a different setting. Thus, lesson environments have to be constructed so that children will perceive that what they have learned in Spanish reading is also applicable in English and vice versa. This suggests that the instruction in the two languages should be closely coordinated, and that planning and teaching for transfer of learning should be included in the training of teachers who work with bilingual children.

Nominal Instructional Program and Reading Achievement

Issue. How is the number of years of enrollment in a Spanish reading program related to reading achievement? In the SEDL study, enrollment in Spanish reading programs was positively related to Spanish reading achievement during the early grades, but this relationship was negligible in the later grades. Children placed in these programs were generally those deemed by the schools to be limited in their English skills with stronger Spanish skills. These children remained in Spanish reading programs until they reached a predetermined level of oral proficiency in English and attained a specified level of reading in Spanish and/or performed above a specified percentile score on an English standardized reading achievement test. Some students received Spanish reading instruction for one year before transfer to English reading; others remained longer, with most being transferred by the end of third grade. Since the oral English skills of most of the students by third-grade exit tended to meet or exceed the oral English criterion for transfer, the few students who remained in Spanish reading programs beyond the third grade were likely those having trouble learning to read.

Consequently, when the entire sample of children were considered, acquired English literacy skills were generally found to be negatively associated with the number of years of enrollment in Spanish reading. However, a separate analysis of the fourth-grade data indicated that, in spite of the transfer criteria, students who had had longer enrollments in Spanish reading programs showed relatively superior English literacy skills. This could be interpreted to mean, as other studies have found (Cummins, 1983; Doebler & Mardis, 1980-1981; González, 1977; Leyba, 1978; Rosier & Farella, 1976; San Diego City Schools, 1982; Troike, 1981; Willig, 1985) that the full benefits of initial reading instruction in the home language often are not apparent until the later elementary grades. This finding may also be related to the unique characteristics of the fourth-grade sample which consisted entirely of students from the US-Mexico border sites where the development of oral bilingual competence was strongly supported in the students' environment. Thus, in keeping with the developmental interdependence hypothesis (Cummins, 1979), which speaks to the question of how first and second language skills are related, the relative superior English literacy skills of these students may be associated with both transfer of literacy skills across languages and the positive effects of a high level of oral language development in two languages.

Implications. The trends in the data raise some interesting questions. For children who begin initial reading instruction in Spanish is there a threshold level that must be reached in Spanish reading for the benefits of such instruction to affect positive growth in English literacy? If so, does it correspond to the level of literacy that monolingual children normally achieve by the end of third grade? Are children in transitional bilingual education programs, where criteria for transfer to English reading is strongly tied to English performance, being kept in Spanish reading programs long enough to attain the requisite literacy skills in Spanish? These questions merit attention as they are central to the controversy surrounding transitional bilingual education.

Quantity and Quality of Instruction

Issue. To what extent does the quantity and quality of the instruction delivered to bilingual children affect reading achievement? Of the many factors affecting student progress in reading, instruction is the one for which the schools have primary responsibility and over which they have the most control. Identifying instructional patterns associated with success and failure, both in the early stages of reading instruction and in subsequent years, is a critical issue surrounding improvement of practices for all children.

Recent educational research, conducted primarily with students from the general school population, but also with bilingual populations, has produced a solid knowledge base allowing educators to point with confidence to characteristics and actions that differentiate between instructional settings in which students successfully master the learning goals set for them and those in which students are less successful. It identifies and describes what effective teachers do and how effective instruction is accomplished in effective schools. Similarly, some of the most eminent reading experts claim that the best teachers in the best schools know how to turn students into proficient readers (Anderson, Hiebert, Scott, & Wilkinson, 1985).

In examining the findings from the SEDL study's instructional data in relation to this knowledge base, factors associated with student academic gains and successful practices in both monolingual and bilingual classrooms included: (a) a strong focus on academic work where time is spent working with textual materials, (b) increased time allocated to reading and academic verbal interaction, (c) greater use of active teaching practices with relatively large amounts of instruction from the teacher, (d) high achievement expectations with the use of tasks of appropriate difficulty level that challenge the student, yet allow consistent success, and (e) efficient classroom management where allocated instructional time is devoted to instruction and major behavioral disorders are minimized.

Additional factors associated with successful bilingual classrooms included: (a) some use of the home language with Limited English Proficient students, and (b) the use of English primarily during English-medium instructional periods and Spanish primarily during Spanish-medium instructional periods.

Factors associated with less student gain in reading, found in both the SEDL bilingual study as well as in research on monolingual students, included: (a) inappropriate amounts of time devoted to decoding instruction, (b) the use of instruction in decoding which is non-explicit with respect to letter-sound pairing, (c) limited attention to explicit instruction in developing vocabulary and higher-order comprehension strategies, (d) ability grouping of students where students assigned to lower groups become locked into an instructional track in which the range of instruction is limited, and (e) extensive use of seatwork assignments where low reading group students spend less of their seatwork time in beneficial ways.

Implications. The classrooms in the SEDL study exhibited several of the characteristics of effective instruction. In the aggregate, such instruction produced approximately a year of growth for a year of instruction in English reading comprehension: Instruction does make a difference.

While the classrooms were similar in many ways, variation was noted in the quality of the dimensions of instruction assessed. This suggests that to ensure effective instruction of all students, certain instructional dimensions need strengthening. Staff development should aim toward training teachers to (a) monitor their own use of language in the classroom and to provide instructional activities which make strong formal language demands on students; (b) make optimal use of textual materials, favoring these over non-textual materials in both direct instruction and independent work; (c) increase instruction in word meaning and higher-order comprehension skills, strengthening such skills through explicit instruction; and (d) evaluate the decoding needs of their students and tailor their instruction on decoding to identified needs, making such instruction explicit and limited to appropriate amounts. In addition, the practice of grouping students for instruction needs careful consideration, not only in terms of optimal size, but also in terms of student membership, permanency of the group once formed, and instructional treatment provided.

Site Characteristics and Reading Achievement

Issue.   To what extent are differences between sites related to reading achievement? The five Texas sites in the SEDL study were selected to achieve variation in several areas (e.g., size, socioeconomic status, degree of urbanicity, concentration of Hispanic students, characteristics of the reading program). Given differing contextual environments, site differences in language and literacy development could be expected. There were fewer differences between sites in English than in Spanish development. Spanish literacy was more advanced at certain of the border sites where substantial non-school support for Spanish was available.

Implications.   Factors outside the school are important in fostering and maintaining development of the non-English home language. Prominent among these are: (a) the locale and the extent to which the language is used in the community and the home, (b) the attitude of the student and others toward the maintenance of Spanish, and (c) the extent to which written materials and formal usage are available to the students in the home language. Without strong support from the home and the community, students in transitional bilingual education programs are unlikely to achieve high levels of literacy in Spanish.

REFERENCES

Anderson, R. C., Hiebert, E. H., Scott, J. A., & Wilkinson, I. A. G. (1985). *Becoming a nation of readers: The report of the Commission on Reading.* Champaign, IL: University of Illinois.

Bruner, J. (1975). Language as an instrument of thought. In A. Davies (Ed.),

Problems of language and learning. London: Heinemann.

Calfee, R. C., & Freedman, S. (1980). *Understanding and comprehending.* Paper presented at the Center for the Study of Reading, University of Illinois, Champaign, IL.

Clarke, M. A. (1981). Reading in Spanish and English: Evidence from adult ESL students. In S. Hudelson (Ed.), *Learning to read in different languages* (pp. 69-85). Washington, DC: Center for Applied Linguistics.

Cummins, J. (1979). Linguistic interdependence and the educational development of bilingual children. *Review of Educational Research, 49,* 222-251.

Cummins, J. (1981). The role of primary language development in promoting educational success for language minority students. In California State Department of Education, *Schooling and language minority students: A theoretical framework* (pp. 3-49). Los Angeles, CA: National Dissemination and Assessment Center.

Cummins, J. (1983). *Policy report: Language and literacy learning in bilingual instruction.* Austin, TX: Southwest Educational Development Laboratory.

Cziko, G. (1980). Language competence and reading strategies: A comparison of first- and second-language oral reading errors. *Language Learning, 30,* 101-116.

Doebler, L. K., & Mardis, L. J. (1980-1981, Winter). Effects of a bilingual education program for Native-American children. *NABE Journal, 5,* 23-28.

Donaldson, M. (1978). *Children's minds.* Glasgow, England: Collins Press.

Goldman, S. R., Reyes, M., & Varnhagen, C. K. (1984). Understanding fables in first and second languages. *NABE Journal, 8,* 35-66.

González, G. A. (1977). *Brownsville Independent School District bilingual education program Title VII: Final report for 1976-1977.* Brownsville, TX: Brownsville Independent School District.

Goodman, K., & Goodman, Y. M. (1978). *Reading of American children whose language is a stable rural dialect of English or a language other than English* (Contract No. NIE-C-00-3-0087). Washington, DC: National Institute of Education.

Klee, C. (1984). *A discourse analysis of the oral language interactions of Spanish/ English bilingual children in three environments.* Unpublished doctoral dissertation, University of Texas at Austin, Austin, TX.

Leyba, C. F. (1978). *Longitudinal study of a Title VII bilingual program, Santa Fe*

Public Schools, Santa Fe, New Mexico. Los Angeles, CA: National Dissemination and Assessment Center.

Matluck, J. H., & Mace-Matluck, B. J. (1981). *A longitudinal study of the acquisition of reading skills by Spanish-English children in the United States.* Paper presented at the 6th World Congress of the International Association of Applied Linguistics, Lund, Sweden.

Mehan, H. (1979). *Learning lessons.* Cambridge: Harvard University Press.

Moll, L. C., Díaz, E., Estrada, E., & Lopes, L. M. (1981). *The construction of learning environments in two languages.* San Diego, CA: Laboratory of Comparative Human Cognition.

Olson, D. R. (1977). From utterance to text: The bias of language in speech and writing. *Harvard Educational Review, 47,* 257-281.

Rosier, P., & Farella, M. (1976). Bilingual education at Rock Point: Some early results. *TESOL Quarterly, 10,* 379-388.

San Diego City Schools. (1982). *ESEA Title VII bilingual demonstration project.* San Diego, CA: Author.

Swain, M. (1981). *Bilingual education for majority and minority language children.* Paper presented at the 6th World Congress of the International Association of Applied Linguistics, Lund, Sweden.

Tregar, B., Brisk, M., Indresano, R., & Lombardo, M. (1981). *The relationship between native language reading comprehension, second language reading comprehension, and second language oral ability.* Unpublished manuscript.

Troike, R. C. (1981). Synthesis of research on bilingual education. *Educational Leadership,* March, 498-504.

Wells, C. G. (1983). *Language at home and at school.* Bristol, England: University of Bristol, School of Education, Centre for the Study of Language and Communication.

Willig, A. C. (1985). A meta-analysis of selected studies on the effectiveness of bilingual education. *Review of Educational Research, 55,* 269-317.

As fellow citizens we need a common language. In the United States this language is English. Our common history is written in English. Our common forefathers speak to us, through the ages, in English.

WILLIAM J. BENNETT
Secretary of Education

12

SPECIAL EDUCATION AND THE CULTURALLY AND LINGUISTICALLY DIFFERENT CHILD:
An Overview of Issues and Challenges

Ann C. Willig

Between the years of 1977 to 1982, enrollment figures for children in special education classes for the learning disabled (LD) more than doubled (Dew, 1984), and most of the children represented by these figures were from minority groups whose culture *and* language differed from that of the dominant Anglo-American society. During and just prior to these increases in the numbers of minority-group children labelled LD, dramatic *decreases* occurred in the numbers of minority-group children placed in classes for the mentally retarded (MR) due to legal decisions and mandates that prohibited discriminatory assessment and placement practices. The increased LD enrollment for culturally and linguistically different children indicates that inappropriate placement of minority students in special education continues and has merely shifted from the category of MR to LD. For example, Dew (1984) cites data showing that of one hundred school districts which appeared to warrant investigation for discrimination in the placement of limited-English-proficient (LEP) children, sixteen districts had placed 100 percent of their LEP students in Special Education classes, and more than forty districts had placed between 50 and 100 percent of their LEP students in special education!

191

Although these data were not available to Dew by special education category, Ortiz and Yates (1983) reported data from Texas that *were* disaggregated by category. Their data indicate that although the proportion of Hispanic students receiving special education services in Texas approximated the proportion in the general population, disaggregation of the figures by special education categories revealed a 300 percent *over*-representation of Hispanic students in LD classes. Furthermore, Hispanics were *under*-represented in every other service category.

This over-representation of culturally and linguistically different children in classes for the learning disabled, along with the underrepresentation in other categories, poses a major issue in the education of minority-group children. The disproportion raises a host of questions and poses a number of challenges for educators and policy makers that concern every facet and every level of service planning and service delivery for language-minority children. This paper provides an overview of some of these issues and challenges. The first of these is the need for accurate demographic information that can provide a planning base for special education services.

PLANNING FOR CURRENT AND
FUTURE NEEDS IN SPECIAL EDUCATION

In order to plan for the future educational needs of linguistic-minority children and to identify malfunctions in the delivery of services to these children, accurate information is needed concerning the numbers of children being served in the various program categories of special education. Furthermore, these figures must be broken down according to the specific cultural and linguistic characteristics of the children. When data are disaggregated in this way, malfunctions in identification and placement systems become apparent, as in the previously-cited figures which suggest that many perfectly normal language-minority children are being labelled LD and placed in special education programs while others, who may truly need special education services, are being passed over in the identification process. Accurate enrollment information also is needed to assess the match of existing resources to needs, and to ensure that adequate numbers of personnel will be trained and available as future needs arise.

The disproportionate special education enrollment figures that have been revealed by the few studies where disaggregated data *were* obtained lead directly to the remaining major issues that surround the education of minority-group children, i.e., *why* are so many minority-group children placed in special education, and is special education really an appropriate alternative for serving minority children who are not achieving academically?

SPECIAL EDUCATION AND THE
LOW–ACHIEVING MINORITY CHILD

There are two major reasons for the current over-representation of minority-group children in classes for the learning disabled, apart from actual overt or covert discrimination. The first concerns the inability of teaching and assessment personnel to distinguish between true language/learning disabilities and the normal process of second language acquisition for a minority-language child. The second, which arises from a sincere desire on the part of local educational personnel to provide assistance for a low-achieving child, is the supposition that a minority-language child who is not succeeding in the regular classroom should be offered special education services to receive extra help with subject matter content and language learning.

There are several reasons why the placement of language-minority children in special education so they can receive extra help is *not* an appropriate alternative. These are reviewed in detail by Cummins (1984) and include the familiar issue of labelling, with its consequent negative effects on the educational career of a child, and the possible inappropriateness of the instructional strategies to be used with a child once he or she is placed in the special education program. Furthermore, placement in special education implies that school failure is due to inadequacies in the *child* when it may very well be due to the nature of the educational instruction that has been provided for the child prior to referral. In fact, serious examination of the nature of instruction that has been received by the child prior to referral may be a major way to reduce the number of inappropriate referrals for special education assessment.

In some districts, referral to special education automatically requires that a classroom observation be done by an educational liaison or other person to determine the exact nature of the child's problem. However, adequate implementation of this process is all too infrequent. The introduction of a pre-referral phase where classroom observations *must* be made and alternative teaching methods *truly tried and documented* would not only reduce the number of inappropriate referrals for assessment, it would also place the onus for academic failure on the institution rather than the child. For the culturally and linguistically different child, such a pre-referral process would require that the cultural and linguistic appropriateness of education also be examined.

ISSUES OF LANGUAGE ASSESSMENT

By far, one of the most critical issues in the education of language-minority children is the determination of language dominance, or *relative language proficiency.* As educational policy currently functions in this country, determination of a child's language proficiency is the basis for one of the most important decisions to be made about any minority child's education — that of the language in which the child will be taught. In federally funded bilingual programs, *English* language proficiency rather than *relative* language proficiency, or language dominance, is usually the deciding factor for placement in bilingual education. For low-achieving minority-language children who are referred for special education assessment, the determination, or even the failure to determine, relative language proficiency plays a central role in determining eligibility for special education services and in designating a label for a child, such as LD or MR. This is due to the fact that the distinction between true disabilities and normal stages of second language acquisition may be revealed through examination of relative language proficiency.

In order to determine whether a language-minority child does indeed have an educational handicap, the child must be tested in his or her strongest language, since a true disability must be apparent in the dominant language. If there is no disability in the child's dominant language, there can be no disability. Any symptoms of disability must then be manifestations of the process of second language acquisition.

The importance of determining a child's language dominance through language proficiency assessments in *both* languages cannot be overemphasized since policies in some districts do not distinguish between *relative* language proficiency and *limited English* proficiency. For example, data collected at the Handicapped Minority Research Institute on Language Proficiency (1984) revealed that language proficiency in English frequently is the sole measure of language that appears in records of language-minority students who have been placed in special education programs. Furthermore, language proficiency information in student folders was frequently found to be out of date, sometimes by several years, an indication that decision-makers are not sufficiently cognizant of the nature and rapidity of language change in children who live in dual language environments. Changes occur not only in the acquisition of the second language but also in loss of the primary language if the child is not in a program that emphasizes the continuation of primary language development.

Although it is important that relative language proficiency be determined through language assessments in at least two languages, those who rely on the results of language assessments must be cognizant of the complexities inherent in language assessment. The fact is that tests of language proficiency generally have low reliability and low convergent validity (see, e.g., Gilmore and Dickenson, 1979; Hoepfner and Coniff, 1974; Rivera and Simich, 1981; Silverman, Noa and Russell, 1977; Troike, 1982; Tucker, 1974). This is due both to the nature of language use at the level of the individual and to the changing nature of theory and practice in language assessment.

At the individual level, patterns of language use vary a great deal depending upon the topic and context of communication. For a child who lives in a dual language environment, certain topics of conversation with certain types of individuals in certain kinds of settings may call forth one language while very different topics with different individuals in different settings are usually dealt with in the other language. For example, topics that are commonly discussed in the home may be quite different from those discussed in school, with peers, or in church, and each of these might normally be conducted in different languages. Consequently, language proficiency in the different *domains* will vary. This almost infinite variety in language use contributes to the low reliability and validity of the tests. In fact, whether a child is categorized as limited-English proficient may be more a function of which test is used than the actual language characteristics of the child (Ulibarri, Spencer and Rivas, 1981).

Also contributing to the lack of convergent validity in language tests is the changing nature of the theoretical underpinnings of language assessment. For example, the basic questions of what language proficiency is, and which aspects of language are most important to language proficiency, are still in a state of controversy. There have been several paradigm shifts in linguistics and psycholinguistics over the past twenty years and each paradigm has emphasized the importance of different aspects of language (see, E.g., Bloomfield, 1933; Chomsky, 1957; Fillmore, 1968; Labov, 1970; Shuy, 1977). The result has been a plethora of tests that demonstrate low convergent validity because of their differential emphases.

In addition to the variation in language use as described above, Cummins (1981, 1984) distinguishes between oral language proficiency as used in interpersonal contexts and proficiency in the type of language that is necessary to academic success and which carries few concrete contextual cues to meaning. The latter type of language requires a broader vocabulary and proficiency in dealing with abstract linguistic messages. The failure to distinguish between oral proficiency and the type of proficiency required for academic success often misleads educators into falsely concluding that a child has acquired adequate second language proficiency to handle instruction that is given in the second language. Cummins (1984) presents data which suggest that it takes an immigrant child approximately two years to acquire oral language skills in their second language and approximately five to seven years to acquire the language skills that are necessary for academic success comparable to that of native language speakers.

In spite of the host of unsolved problems that exist in the area of language assessment, the fact is that every day crucial decisions are made about the educational careers of minority language children. Given the impact that knowledge or ignorance of the child's language characteristics will have on the outcomes of these decisions, it is essential that language proficiency be assessed in *both* languages. The safest course would seem to be in the employment of several types of tests with each child so that patterns of results can be examined and utilized in decisions concerning the child. Carpenter (1984) points to a growing concensus among linguists that the determination of relative language proficiency should include a comprehensive assessment of language which uses natural language samples acquired in various settings. Information collected through these assessments should probably be reported separately by domain, given the variation of language proficiency across domains. Mace-Matluck and Hoover (1986) conducted a longitudinal study of LEP children from grades K-4 which included language testing. They write:

> Analyses of the oral language data strongly suggest that none of the existing measures by themselves provides adequate information on which to base educational decisions. Use of a variety of types of measures and procedures can, however, provide a reasonably accurate index of the students' oral language abilities (p. 15).

The complexity of the language proficiency issue affects not only decisions concerning the language to be used for assessment and instructions, it also interacts with various aspects of cognitive assessment.

COGNITIVE ASSESSMENT OF
LANGUAGE MINORITY CHILDREN

The central issue in assessing minority-language children for learning disabilities lies in making the distinction between a learning/language disorder and manifestations of second language learning. Many child characteristics that are considered to be symptomatic of a learning disability in monolingual children are so closely related to language that, when applied to children trying to function in an unfamiliar language, they simply describe aspects of the second language learning situation. For example, the normal errors made by second language learners in syntax, articulation and vocabulary are frequently defined as communication disorders in the absence of knowledge about the second language learning process. Other children are referred for special education assessment due to distractibility or lack of attention in the classroom. These behaviors may simply reflect that the children do not understand the language sufficiently to be motivated to attend to what is being said. Poor comprehension and/or inability to follow directions is another common referral reason, again one that may directly reflect the child's lack of familiarity with the language of the teacher. Cummins (1984) calls attention to the lack of validity of tests used to identify learning disabilities in monolingual contexts and emphasizes the necessity for extreme caution when interpreting tests conducted in bilingual contexts.

The importance of the determination of relative language proficiency in deciding the language of assessment has already been addressed. However, if a minority-language child has been instructed primarily in English for any length of time, testing in the native language may *not* be appropriate due to the degree of language loss in the first language (L1) or the failure to develop the academic language abilities in L1 that are required by the testing situation. Cummins (1984) suggests that after two years of monolingual education in the second language, testing should not be conducted in the native language.

It appears that the determining factor for any type of assessment to be done with a language minority child is the relative language proficiency of the child *in the domain that matches that of the tests to be used.* The confusing consequence of adherence to this principle is that academic language proficiency is probably best measured with academic achievement tests, and these are frequently the very tests that are the object of the assessment.

A second major issue in the assessment of cultural and

linguistic minorities has been that of the cultural bias of principal tests used. PL 94-142 requires that the materials and procedures used for the assessment of learning handicaps should not be discriminatory due to race or culture and that the instruments should be valid for the purpose for which they are used. Cummins (1984 and in this issue) presents a cogent discussion of ways in which test bias is built into the test construction and norming of the Wechsler Intelligence Scale for Children, the test that is most commonly used as one of the components of assessment for learning disabilities.

A number of alternatives to increase the validity of cognitive and language tests for minority group children have been attempted. For example, tests have been normed on populations outside of the United States or off the mainland, such as Mexico or Puerto Rico, but the applicability of these norms is inadequate for children born and raised in a dual language environment and whose primary language is a minority language which holds a relatively low status. Translations of tests have been used but these, too, are found to be wanting in that they usually do not reflect the dialect of the child. Some researchers (e.g., Mercer, 1973), have devised ways to adjust test scores for sociocultural differences in children who take the tests. These scores, however, do not have predictive validity for the children because the educational system remains unchanged (Cummins, 1984). Attempts to devise culture free tests have also proved to be problematical since, as Cummins (1984) points out, *culture* free is the equivalent of *experience* free. The use of local test norms, or information that reflects characteristics of particular types of children, is one way in which assessment might afford diagnostic value.

At present, promising techniques for determining a child's learning ability are tests devised to measure problem solving behavior, such as the Kaufman ABC (Kaufman and Kaufman, 1982) or to determine mediated learning ability as with the Feuerstein LPAD (Feuerstein, 1979).

ISSUES IN INSTRUCTION

As many authors have pointed out, the single most important question concerning the outcome of the referral and assessment process is whether or not the individual educational needs of the child are ultimately met. In spite of the requirements for Individualized Instructional Programs, administrators and decision-making personnel frequently are under the mistaken impression that bilingual education and special education are mutually exclusive and they are seen as alternatives to each other. If a child receives special education, he or she is not believed to be eligible for bilingual education, and vice versa. Although bilingual special education has no legal mandate defining it as a separate program of instruction, bilingual education for children of limited-English proficiency is encouraged by federal law as a means of providing educational opportunities for these children that are as effective as those provided to children whose primary language is English. Furthermore, laws in many states *require* that bilingual education programs be offered to children of limited-English proficiency. These requirements, coupled with the requirements of PL 94-142 that the unique educational needs of each child be met, lay the groundwork for bilingual special education or for various arrangements whereby a child will receive native language instruction according to his or her needs. Unfortunately, the failure to acknowledge the linguistic needs of language minority children is more prevalent than not.

One reason for the failure to consider alternative languages for instruction rests in a frequently-encountered philosophy among special educators that if a child has problems that impede learning, dual language instruction will only lead to cognitive confusion. Reasoning that the language the child will need most is English, special educators submerge language-minority children in English-language instructional programs. This approach has not worked with nonhandicapped minority-language children, as evidenced by the high drop-out rates of such children from school (66 percent in the case of Hispanics), and pure logic dictates that English language submersion would be even less successful with children who have learning handicaps. If, indeed, the child has a problem that impedes learning, then it makes much more sense to teach the child in the language that the child understands best. There is considerable evidence that bilingual instruction for non-handicapped children improves academic achievement in English as well as in academic subjects taught in the native language (see, e.g., Cummins, 1981, 1984; Troike, 1978; Willig, 1985, for reviews of this evidence) and there is growing evidence concerning the success of dual and native language instruction for limited-English-proficient children who have learning handicaps (Baca and Bransford, 1982; Cummins, 1984; Ortiz, 1984).

Although instruction in the native language is a logical and valid alternative for children in special education programs, determination of the optimal language of instruction often becomes quite complex. This complexity is illustrated by one type of situation that could easily be overlooked in the process

203

of planning IEPs. Data from the Handicapped Minority Research Institute in Texas (1985) revealed a number of Hispanic children whose home language surveys indicated that both English and Spanish were spoken in the home but that English was the predominant language. Children from these homes might *understand* Spanish but may never have *spoken* in any language other than English. On tests of English proficiency, however, the children would score low enough to be considered "limited-English proficient." *In the absence of concomitant language testing in Spanish,* with a process sensitive enough to detect the actual English monolingualism or dominance, as the case may be, the child might be placed in a situation of Spanish language instruction when, in fact, English language instruction might have been more appropriate. Again, sensitive language assessment in both languages is essential information for the decisions that must be made concerning the education of language-minority students.

There are other issues that concern the nature of the educational program that results from the assessment and placement of a child in special education. The first concerns the notion that special education programs provide individualized instruction that is designed to meet the unique needs of each child. The fact is, in many special education programs, instruction is no more individualized than in regular classrooms. Frequently, pupil-teacher ratios are no different in special education classrooms than in regular classrooms, and there is usually greater heterogeneity in the special education room. Resource rooms often contain students from three or four different grade levels at one time with only one teacher and sometimes an aide. Individualized instruction in this type of setting is extremely difficult and many teachers solve the problem by teaching all of the children the same thing at the same time. Self-contained classrooms may be even more heterogeneous because of the aggregation of children who are diagnosed as mentally retarded and those who are considered to be emotionally disturbed. Additionally, these classrooms also contain children from many different grade levels. A major challenge for special educators is to truly provide individualized instruction according to the needs of the child. Ways must be found to assist teachers in carrying out individualized programs and adequate personnel must be provided to allow this to happen.

A final issue in the education of children both in special education and in regular education centers on the nature of the instructional process. Cummins (1984) contrasts two approaches to education in making the point that many of the problems that are labelled learning disabilities may actually be rooted in educational methodology rather than in the child. Direct transmission models, which have characterized traditional education, rely on transmitting the rules of any given learning task in discrete steps and in separate units which carry little relevance for the child. Motivation for learning in this setting is extrinsic and must be instilled through manipulations of the teachers. Cummins contrasts direct instruction with reciprocal interaction models which are based on the concept of learning as a process of constructing one's own knowledge. One example he uses in describing the reciprocal interaction model is the learning of one's first language—a child figures out the rules of language through constant interaction with others and gradually approximates adult norms, all without explicit instruction in language. Intrinsic motivation for learning language is maintained by the fact that learning language serves an immediate and useful purpose for the child. Cummins contends that reading and writing would be more effectively learned if taught in accord with these principles. Flores, Rueda and Porter (in this issue) support this contention with a cogent example of the interaction model used for writing instruction.

It is Cummins' contention that the prevalence of the direct transmission model may be the source of the overwhelming numbers of children who have problems in the educational setting. If this is so (and the issue lies open to research), then instruction in special education settings is especially open to criticism since the use of task analyses and the teaching of discrete units of instruction is a common methodology in special education.

As can be seen from the issues reviewed in this paper, we have much to learn concerning the provision of an appropriate education for children whose language and culture differ from that which predominates in our society. The challenges are clear. Issues concerning the referral, assessment, placement and instruction of minority-group children must be addressed at all levels, by individual teachers, assessment personnel, administrative personnel, policy-making bodies, and researchers who can help to unravel some of the complexity that characterizes these issues.

REFERENCES

Baca, L. & Bransford, J. (1982). *An Appropriate Education for Handicapped Children of Limited English Proficiency.* Reston, VA: ERIC Clearinghouse on Handicapped and Gifted Children.

Baecher, R. E. (1981). Language proficiency assessment: Issues and definitions. In

Stanley S. Seidner (Ed.), *Issues of Language Assessment: Foundations and Research.* Springfield, IL: Illinois State Board of Education.

Bloomfield, L. (1933). *Language.* New York: Holt, Rinehart and Winston.

Carpenter, L. J. (1983). *Bilingual Special Education: An Overview of Issues.* Los Alamitos, CA: National Center for Bilingual Research.

Chomsky, N. (1957). *Syntactic Structures.* The Hague: Mouton.

Chomsky, N. (1965). *Aspects of the Theory of Syntax.* Cambridge, MA: M.I.T. Press.

Cummins, J. (1981). The role of primary language development in promoting educational success for language minority students. In California State Department of Education (Ed.), *Schooling and Language Minority Students: A Theoretical Framework.* Los Angeles, CA: National Dissemination and Assessment Center.

Cummins, J. (1984). *Bilingualism and Special Education.* Clevedon, England: Multilingual Matters.

Dew, N. (1984). The exceptional bilingual child: Demography. In P. C. Chinn (Ed.), *Education of Culturally and Linguistically Different Exceptional Children.* Reston, VA: Council for Exceptional Children.

Fillmore, C. J. (1968). The case for case. In E. Bach and R. T. Harms (Eds.), *Universals in Linguistic Theory.* New York: Holt, Rinehart and Winston.

Feuerstein, R. (1979). *The Dynamic Assessment Of Retarded Performers: The Learning Potential Assessment Device, Theory, Instruments and Techniques.* Baltimore, MD: University Part press.

Gilmore, G., & Dickenson, A. (1979). *The Relationship Between Instruments Used for Identifying Children of Limited English Speaking Ability in Texas.* Houston, TX: Region IV Education Service Center.

Handicapped Minority Research Institute on Language Proficiency (1985). *Technical Report #1A.* Austin, TX: Department of Special Education, University of Texas.

Hoepfner, R., & Coniff, W., Jr. (Eds.) (1974). *CSF Secondary School Test Evaluations: Grades 7 and 8.* Los Angeles, CA: University of California, Center for the Study of Evaluation, Evaluation Technologies Program.

Kaufman, A. S. & Kaufman, N. L. (1982). *Kaufman Assessment Battery for Children: Interpretive Manual.* Circle Pines, MN: American Guidance Service.

Labov, W. (1970). *The Study of Nonstandard English.* Urbana, IL: National Council of Teachers of English.

Mace-Matluck, B., Hoover, W., & Calfee, R. (1985). *Language, Literacy, and Instruction in Bilingual Settings: A K-4 Longitudinal Study*. Austin, TX: Southwest Education Development Laboratory.

Mercer, J. R. (1973). *Labelling the Mentally Retarded*. Los Angeles, CA: University of California Press.

Nuttall, E. V., Landurand, P. M., & Goldman, P. (1984). A critical look at testing and evaluation from a cross-cultural perspective. In P. C. Chinn (Ed.), *Education of Culturally and Linguistically Different Exceptional Children*. Reston, VA: Council for Exceptional Children.

Ortiz, A. A. (1984). Language and curriculum development for exceptional bilingual children. In P. C. Chinn (Ed.), *Education of Culturally and Linguistically Different Exceptional Children*. Reston, VA: Council for Exceptional Children.

Ortiz, A. A. & Yates, J. R. (1983). Incidence of exceptionality among Hispanics: Implications for Manpower Planning. *NABE Journal*, 7, 41-54.

Rivera, C., & Simich, C. (1981). Language proficiency assessment: Research findings and their application. In S. A. Seidner (Ed.), *Issues of Language Assessment: Foundations and Research*. Springfield, IL: Illinois State Board of Education.

Roos, P. D. (Undated). *The Handicapped, Limited-English-proficient Student: A School District's Obligation*. Coral Gables, FL: National Origin Desegregation Assistance Center.

Shuy, R. (1977). Quantitative language data: A case for and some warnings against. *Anthropology in Education Quarterly*, 8(2), 73-82.

Silverman, R. J., Noa, J. K., & Russell, R. H. (1977). *Oral Language Tests for Bilingual Students: An Evaluation of Language Dominance and Proficiency Instruments*. Portland, OR: Northwest Regional Educational Laboratory.

Troike, R. C. (1978). Research evidence for the effectiveness of bilingual education. *NABE Journal*, 3(1), 13-24.

Troike, R. C. (1982). Zeno's paradox and language assessment. In S. S. Seidner (Ed.), *Issues of Language Assessment: Foundations and Research*. Springfield, IL: Illinois State Board of Education.

Tucker, G. R. (1974). The assessment of bilingual and bicultural factors of communication. In S. T. Carey (Ed.), *Bilingualism, Biculturalism and Education*. Edmonton: University of Alberta Press.

Ulibarri, D. M., Spencer, M. L., & Rivas, G. A. (1981). Language proficiency and academic achievement: A study of language proficiency tests and their relationship to school ratings as predictors of academic achievement. *NABE Journal, V*(3), 47-80.

Willig, A. C. (1985). A meta-analysis of selected studies on the effectiveness of bilingual education. *Review of Educational Research,* Fall.

INDEX